"The baton is being passed, handed-off preach the truth that we cannot be righteous in our own strength. Kenneth will be one of those men impacting this emerging generation; encouraging believers, reverently expositing the Scriptures, and combating false emergent teachings. His voice will be influential, not just within our own movement but also across the spectrum of Christianity. I am confident that the teaching and preaching of Kenneth Ortiz will give you insights that will help you as you seek to allow the Lord to intervene in your own life, so God can do the work in you that you could not do for yourself."

—**Chuck Smith**, founder of the *Calvary Chapel* movement

"*Redefined* is vintage Kenneth Ortiz. I have known Ortiz for many years. He has developed a strong reputation of teaching and writing about theology in a way that regular folks can understand. But more than just being a good teacher of theology, he has proven to be a man of integrity and he loves people the way a good pastor should. I highly recommend his book."

—**James Pitman**, director of advancement, Dallas Theological Seminary

"In *Redefined*, Kenneth Ortiz takes a careful and reverent approach to teaching several essential Christian doctrines. He does it so well that he'll satisfy even the most savvy Biblical scholars, but he also writes simply enough that the non-scholars can fully understand the Biblical concepts that he presents. I especially appreciate Kenneth's commitment to exposing the bad thinking that many believers suffer from. This book will remind you of the power of the gospel and the immense love of God."

—**Philip Taylor**, executive pastor at Mosaic Church in Orlando, FL, and regional coordinator for *The Acts 29* Network

"This is one of the most transformational books I have ever read. Finally, someone writes with clarity and accuracy about what we gain through Christ in salvation. Get ready to breathe new life and understanding as you dive deep through the pages of stories and sound doctrine that will change you forever. I highly recommend this book to all new and seasoned believers who endeavor to fully grasp how to live the Christian life!"

—**Jimn Kyles**, lead pastor at the CHURCH in Rosenberg, TX, and church planters' coach for Association of Related Churches (ARC)

"With a high view of the Word and a passion for people, Kenneth Ortiz takes theology out of seminaries and brings it to the every person, reminding us each step of the way that God has redefined our identity through the perfect love of his son, Jesus. *Redefined* is a gift for anyone who struggles to understand how God sees them, and assures us that no matter how we feel about ourselves, God's label is the only one that truly lasts."

—**Aubrey Sampson**, author of *Shameless: Kick Down Your House of Lies and Become the Woman God Designed You to Be*

"There are several key doctrines every believer needs to understand if they are to experience genuine intimacy with Christ. In *Redefined*, Kenneth Ortiz eloquently examines justification by faith and the imputation of Christ's righteousness in a fun and balanced way. He makes these concepts easy to grasp and helps believers understand and embrace the incredible freedom we now have through Christ. I highly recommend this book to every person who follows Jesus."

—**Kenneth Freire**, student discipleship director at Bethany College of Missions, Bloomington, MN

"*Redefined* is a clear explanation of why the gospel is such *good news!* Kenneth unpacks timeless Biblical truths with relevant examples, stories, and illustrations to give his readers a rich understanding of the love of God, our imputed righteousness, full justification, and adoption into God's family. This book will remind you of the power and beauty of the gospel. I'm truly excited to get it into the hands of our church."

—**Gabriel Forsyth**, pastor of discipleship & mission, Mosaic Church in Oakland, FL, and regional coordinator for *The GCM Collective*

"Funny, challenging, motivational, awesome. There aren't enough adjectives to describe how good Kenneth is when he's got the microphone in his hand. As a speaker, he is dynamic! And now the world gets his thoughts in book form?!? What a treat! If you want to know more about the love of God and stop feeling worthless, then read this book today!"

—**James Roach**, audio engineer for musical artist *Guns-n-Roses*

"Kenneth Ortiz is a powerhouse of ministry and leadership. He brings words of wisdom and a challenge for you to be a real disciple of Jesus. Kenneth's words will help you explore the depth and greatness of God's love and grace."

—**Lisa Howard**, MA, school administrator & counselor, Jefferson City, MO

Redefined

Redefined

Discovering and Celebrating What God Really Thinks of You

Kenneth Ortiz

Foreword by Shannon Ethridge

LEAFWOOD
PUBLISHERS

REDEFINED

Discovering and Celebrating What God Really Thinks of You

LEAFWOOD
PUBLISHERS

Copyright © 2014 by Kenneth Ortiz

ISBN 978-0-89112-499-3 | 2013049260

Scripture quotations, unless otherwise noted, are from The Holy Bible, English Standard Version® (ESV®), copyright © 2001 by Crossway, a publishing ministry of Good News Publishers. Used by permission. All rights reserved.

Scripture quotations noted KJV are taken from the King James Version of the Bible.

Scriptures noted NKJV are taken from the New King James Version. Copyright © 1982 by Thomas Nelson, Inc. Used by permission. All rights reserved.

Scripture quotations marked NIV are taken from The Holy Bible, New International Version®, NIV®. Copyright ©1973, 1978, 1984, 2011 by Biblica, Inc.™ Used by permission of Zondervan. All rights reserved worldwide.

Scripture quotations noted NLT are taken from the New Living Translation, copyright ©1996, 2004. Used by permission of Tyndale House Publishers, Inc., Carol Stream, IL 60188. All rights reserved.

Scripture quotations marked "PHILLIPS" are taken from The New Testament in Modern English, copyright © 1958, 1959, 1960 J.B. Phillips and 1947, 1952, 1955, 1957 The Macmillian Company, New York. Used by permission. All rights reserved.

Scripture quotations noted MSG taken from *The Message*. Copyright 1993, 1994, 1995, 1996, 2000, 2001, 2002. Used by permission of NavPress Publishing Group.

Published in association with the Seymour Agency, 475 Miner Street Road, Canton, NY 13617.

Author's Note: Herein I share a variety of personal stories. All of the stories are accurate; however, several names have been changed to protect privacy.

LIBRARY OF CONGRESS CATALOGING-IN-PUBLICATION DATA

Ortiz, Kenneth E., 1982-
  Redefined : discovering and celebrating what God really thinks of you / Kenneth E. Ortiz ; foreword by Shannon Ethridge.
    pages cm
  ISBN 978-0-89112-499-3
  1. Salvation--Christianity. 2. Christian life. I. Title.
  BT752.O78 2014
  248.4--dc23

                                                                    2013049260

Cover design by Marc Whitaker | Interior text design by Sandy Armstrong, Strong Design

For information contact:
Abilene Christian University Press
1626 Campus Court | Abilene, Texas 79601

1-877-816-4455 | www.leafwoodpublishers.com

                 14 15 16 17 18 19 / 7 6 5 4 3 2 1

To Robin Roach

Only God could have foreseen that those

Wednesday night dinners would lead to this.

Acknowledgments

My King and Rescuer Jesus Christ, to whom I owe everything, thank you for redefining how the Father sees me!

My mama, you are the most caring, thoughtful, and considerate person I know. You have been one of my greatest inspirations and one of my best friends. Without you, I would not be the man I am today. Thank you! I love you!

My father, as I get older, I realize more and more how I've become like you, in so many ways, and I wouldn't ever want to change that.

Jimn Kyles, you are like a brother to me! There are no words to express the gratitude I have for our friendship and your constant encouragement.

Shannon Ethridge, thank you for your mentorship! You have been a huge resource for me and an even bigger encouragement to me. It's time to BLAST off!

Jim Roach, thank you for the years of friendship. I have thoroughly enjoyed our many breakfast get-togethers and our many crazy adventures!

Joel Coffman, thank you for believing in me and inviting me into your world. No words can express how incredibly grateful I am to be a part of the community and mission of Mosaic.

Renaut van der Riet and the leadership of Mosaic Church, thank you for letting me be a part of the story.

My agent Mary Sue Seymour, thank you for helping to make this project a reality.

Leonard Allen and Gary Myers of Leafwood Publishers, thank you for taking a chance on this unknown author. I am extremely grateful.

My editors Mary Hardegree and Robyn Burwell, thank you for carefully correcting my words. This book is far better than it otherwise would have been because of your efforts and insights.

Shannon Albert, Peter Douglas, and Zooie Arnold, thank you for your research, feedback, and editorial help.

And to all those individuals who have profoundly impacted my life along the way: huge thanks to all of you. You will share in the fruit of this book!

Contents

Foreword

by Shannon Ethridge

"What does God think of me?" "How does God define who I am?" Sadly, many Christians answer these questions in a manner that is devastating to their own emotional and spiritual health.

As the author of the Every Woman's Battle series, and several other books on the topic of healthy sexuality, I've often been the person hearing "true confessions" from Christians about their struggles. I am honored and humbled to have the opportunity to counsel and advise so many people. I find it interesting that so many individuals assume they shouldn't struggle in the ways they do because they're somehow supposed to be "exempt" as Christians. Through these ministry experiences I have discovered an alarming trend: countless sincere Christians are simply unaware of how God sees them and lack understanding of the depth of the power of God at work in their lives.

Believing the wrong things about how God views you can be far more damaging than most people ever realize.

Most Christians I have encountered really do try to live right; but along the journey we Christians take a wrong turn and end up in some sin that we promised ourselves we wouldn't fall into anymore. This often leads to great discouragement.

We struggle with temptation, addictions, guilt, shame, low self-esteem, depression, and bitterness for a wide variety of reasons. We're no different from the rest of the world when it comes to the trials and tribulations we face. However, we are supposed to be very different in how we respond to all of these pressures. God calls us to live differently. We have the ability to walk with an extra spring in our step, birthed from an uncommon confidence in our Creator. We hold the power to overcome any temptation or trial, to control any addiction or affliction, to conquer anything that comes against us. . . . We have the power of God!

Then, why don't we live differently? So many of us are unable to harness this power and live up to the Bible's standards because we've never fully understood what God thinks of us and what God says about us.

That is why it is my absolute privilege to introduce this incredible book. It is written by an author who has proven he has the knowledge that will greatly help you, but more importantly, an author who absolutely loves seeing Christians experience the fullness of the love and grace of God. I believe many

Christians are unable to live full lives because they've never fully understood the concepts Kenneth covers in this book.

Redefined is brilliant! I can assure you, by the time you finish reading this book you're going to be oh-so-grateful for Kenneth's insight, wit, and wisdom. He passionately and eloquently covers several essential biblical concepts that will revolutionize your life, if you embrace them.

I shudder to think what healthier choices I could have made in my life had I read this book in my teens or early twenties. Perhaps I wouldn't have felt the need to look for love in all the wrong places. Maybe I would have realized the magnitude of God's unconditional love for me, and how the love of any other human simply pales in comparison. Maybe I wouldn't have donned a Scarlet Letter on my sweater for so many years, wallowing in the guilt and shame that comes part and parcel with sexual sin. If I had read this book sooner, perhaps I would have felt far more welcome in my Heavenly Bridegroom's presence, because I'd have known I was fully justified ("just-if-I'd" never sinned at all).

If this book had been available to me sooner, maybe I would have recognized the enormous power and strength available to me to overcome my sin, my insecurities, and my addiction to sex. If I had read this book sooner, I would have understood that God defines me as righteous and I don't have to work so hard to earn his approval . . . because God already lovingly approves of me. If I had embraced the concepts in this book sooner, I would have understood the concept of God's unconditional love and unmerited favor and grace in a far greater manner, and that would have undoubtedly transformed my life.

Fortunately, the Holy Spirit has brought these concepts to life for me through many years of reading and researching, fasting and praying . . . and seeking, and seeking, and seeking some more . . . repenting, repeating my dysfunctional patterns, and then repenting again, only to find God unwavering in his commitment to my sanctification process. And only by his mercy and grace has my greatest misery evolved into my greatest ministry.

Now, it is my greatest joy to coach others through a similar process, and I am delighted to have this book as a sharp tool in my ministry tool belt. I credit Kenneth Ortiz for helping me become an even more effective minister to others.

In 2009, I launched a mentorship program called BLAST (Building Leaders, Authors, Speakers, and Teachers). Kenneth was one of the first students to apply to the program, and I could tell that he possessed enormous potential. I actually remember thinking, "As a communicator, this guy is on the cusp of greatness!"

Each time he delivered a speech, my suspicion was confirmed. He was soon recognized by the entire class as "the cream of the crop." Everyone eagerly anticipated his presentations, not just because he was such a dynamic communicator, but because we knew he would challenge, encourage, inspire, and even entertain us . . . and make it all look effortless on his part. *Kenneth is the kind of speaker that I call "poetry in motion," and it's so evident that he moves to the rhythms of God's grace.*

I'll never forget the class when Kenneth was asked to make a presentation on that very topic—grace. He told a story he'd heard about the difference between a police officer and an ambulance driver.

Both a police officer and an ambulance driver arrive on the scene of an accident wanting to know what's happened. However, they have very different motives. The police officer wants to know, "Who is to blame? Who deserves to be punished?" But the ambulance driver simply wants to know, "Who's hurt? Who needs attention?"

Kenneth challenged us to be "ambulance driver Christians" rather than "police officer Christians." Indeed, to show the genuine love of Christ, we need to be less concerned with blame and punishment, and more concerned with care and compassion.

Every time I'm in a life coaching session with a woman or a married couple and I hear what kind of wreck their lives have become, that word picture comes to mind. I'm not a "police officer" coach. I'm not looking for who is to blame. I'm an "ambulance driver" coach. I also try to be an ambulance driver speaker and an ambulance driver writer. I want to be used by God to stop the spiritual bleeding and bring deep healing. This has given me a crystal-clear lens through which to view my role in people's lives, and I'm so grateful to Kenneth for how this memorable concept has impacted my entire life and ministry.

Kenneth told me his goal was to "help Christians discover the right things to believe, both about God and also about themselves." Well, Kenneth has achieved his goal. But more than just teaching doctrines and concepts, Kenneth's pastoral love for people abundantly bleeds through these pages. This book is obviously a "work of love."

If you follow Jesus, then Kenneth's words will help you understand where you stand with God—bringing clarity to how Jesus has redefined your status in the family of God and restored your ability to have intimate communion for our Heavenly Father. God exchanged your old nature for a new nature. If you are not a follower of Jesus, this book may not appear to be written for you, but I eagerly encourage you to continue reading; Kenneth's thoughts will give you great insight into the character of God, specifically his incredible love for all of humanity—yourself included!

Redefined is not a self-help book; this book is unapologetically a theology book! But the cool thing about this book is that it's not a nerdy theology book. Many theology books are hard to understand and written for astute scholars, but *Redefined* is a theology book written for ordinary folks, just like

> *Redefined* is not a self-help book; this book is unapologetically a theology book! But the cool thing about this book is that it's not a nerdy theology book.

you and me. Kenneth has presented some deep and profound doctrinal concepts, but he has done so in a fun and exciting way that will inspire you. He has worked really hard to eliminate the "nerd factor" as much as possible, but has still given us the biblical "meat" we need to be all God calls us to be.

Redefined is jam-packed with Kenneth's trademark friendly intimacy and with dynamic illustrations from Hollywood films and several heart-warming stories that you will absolutely love and never forget—just like I've never forgotten his ambulance driver analogy.

I have tremendous confidence that the timeless truths that Kenneth presents about God's character and nature—and our rich inheritances as God's beloved children—will be brought to life for you in a supernatural way as you peruse these pages. And as you read, I pray you also develop a whole new lens through which to view our blessed Savior and yourself as his fallen-yet-still-faithful follower.

—Shannon Ethridge, MA
www.shannonethridge.com
www.blastmentoring.com

Chapter 1

The New Creation

A few summers ago I was spending time with family in my mother's backyard. It was a hot and humid day, like many that residents of New Jersey endure. Ordinarily, I would never spend this much time outside of an air conditioned room during the month of August, but my younger sister, Brianna—nearly twenty years younger than I—was on a mission, and she needed an accomplice. Her goal was to catch a particular creature. A creature she believed to be the most beautiful she had ever seen.

We darted around the yard with cup-shaped hands, pouncing on each one that we saw; but they were often faster than we were. A few times, our awkward attempts landed us in the bushes. But finally, after much effort, we caught one. Brianna was absolutely enamored. With a contagious smile lighting up her face, she shouted, "Look Kenny, a bubber-bly!"

Finally, we had one in our grasps. We examined it carefully. Large wings with an array of oranges and yellows, trimmed with what seemed to be white polka dots, and laced with black and orange stripes. It felt as if we were looking through a kaleidoscope. What brilliance! What beauty! What a find! There are few things in life that can bring such joy to the heart of a young girl as the beauty of this small flying insect—the monarch butterfly.

The butterfly is the result of a caterpillar that has undergone a transformation. Something happens to the caterpillar after it has spun itself into its chrysalis. The caterpillar exchanges its old nature for a completely new one.

Caterpillars are very different from butterflies in many ways. Caterpillars have limited senses and rely on their short, underdeveloped antennae, so they don't travel far from wherever they were born.

The monarch butterfly, on the other hand, has an uncanny homing system that allows it to migrate thousands of miles south for the winter. Monarch migration is one of the greatest marvels of science. Some researchers have tracked these butterflies from the Great Lakes region of the United States to central Mexico, and then all the way back home to the exact same tree on which it had spun its chrysalis the previous year. This is an amazing accomplishment, especially when I consider how often I can't even find my own car in the mall parking lot.

The caterpillar is marvelously transformed; and as a result of this transformation, the caterpillar is completely redefined. Before its time in the chrysalis, the caterpillar is defined as a larva. But afterward, the caterpillar is defined very differently. We don't ever see a butterfly and say to ourselves, "Oh look, an adult caterpillar!" No! Of course not! When we see the butterfly, we often don't even consider the caterpillar. Most of us never identify the butterfly with the caterpillar.

> Every genuine follower of Jesus is defined by God as a *new creation!*

Brianna doesn't have the same type of relationship with caterpillars as she does with butterflies. In many ways, caterpillars are repulsive to her. She sees a caterpillar and says, "Ewwwww! Gross!" But the caterpillar undergoes a unique transformation, and that transformation causes Brianna to completely redefine her opinion of the creature. She doesn't see the two creatures in the same manner, and she doesn't treat them the same, either. She's elated when she sees butterflies! She loves them; they warm her heart. She longs to delight in the butterfly, and enjoy its beauty.

This isn't much different from how God interacts with humanity. Like the butterfly, the Christian has undergone a transformation. Each person who has genuinely come to believe in God and is sincerely committed to following Jesus has already been fully transformed. The Apostle Paul wrote about this amazing transformation: "Therefore, if anyone is in Christ, he is a new creation. The old has passed away; behold, the new has come" (2 Cor. 5:17). Every genuine follower of Jesus is defined by God as a *new creation!* You are not redefined as merely a better version of your old self—you're not just some fixed-up variety. You are defined as being completely *new!*

Why Do We Need to Be Redefined?

Some might ask, "Why do I need to be redefined?" That is a great question. To answer it, we go back to the very beginning of humanity.

God created Adam and Eve. Human beings were created by God to have perfect friendship with God, free to enjoy and delight in God and in his goodness. We were made in the image of God, endowed with elements of God's character, created to reflect the goodness of God to each other. In the beginning, humanity was in right standing with God. We were created with free access to God. Nothing separated us from him. God saw us as pure and innocent and righteous. We were on God's *good side.* We were defined as his friends, labeled as his children. We had the opportunity to freely walk and talk with God.

But something monumental happened: humanity chose to rebel against God! Adam and Eve disobeyed God's command (Gen. 3:6–7) and all of humanity—every human being since that moment—has followed in their footsteps (Rom. 3:9–10, 23). We sinned!

The consequences of sin cannot be overstated! Sin has poisoned our hearts and grossly corrupted human nature. Sin causes humanity to no longer be in right standing with God. Sin causes God to view us as impure, guilty, and unrighteous. Humanity is on God's *bad side.*

Sin effectively redefined humanity!

Each human being is still endowed with the elements of God's character, but those elements have been severely marred. We now have boundaries between God and us. Because of sin, we were redefined as the enemies of God (Rom. 5:10; Col. 1:21) and labeled as the children of wrath (Eph. 2:3). Tragically, we lost the right to walk and talk with our Creator.

In separating ourselves from God, we brought upon ourselves all of the grief we now face in this life. Disease, pain, strife, heartbreak, stress, depression, corruption, betrayal, shame, loneliness, insecurities . . . all the result of sin. We are guilty, and as such, we deserve to suffer these consequences. Our sinful choices cultivate inside of us appetites for even more sin and wickedness, which causes us to make more sinful choices—a vicious cycle that continually devastates our lives.

Even more horrifying is the possibility that our separation from God will continue beyond this lifetime. Any human being who dies apart from God will be separated from God in a literal lake of fire (Matt. 25:41; Rev. 20:14). Sin devastates our lives and dooms our eternal destinies.

We need to be rescued. Sin redefined us. If we are to ever have a friendship with God again, we must be redefined. Enter stage right: the passionate love of God!

The Rescue Plan

There is a huge difference between God and my sister Brianna—a massive difference between how Brianna sees caterpillars and how God sees sinful humanity. The little girl is hardly capable of seeing beyond the caterpillar's current repulsive state. She doesn't understand that the caterpillar has the potential to be beautiful. But God is both able and willing to see beyond the sinful state of humanity.

God chooses to see our potential. The Creator looks beyond our depravity, choosing to love us in spite of our rebellious ways. God desires to demonstrate his love and grace:

> The LORD is merciful and gracious,
>> slow to anger and abounding in steadfast love.
> He does not deal with us according to our sins,
>> nor repay us according to our iniquities. (Ps. 103:8, 10)

The story could have easily ended after we sinned. God could have allowed the story to end with our eternal damnation. God was under no obligation to rescue humanity. But he has chosen not to treat us as we deserve. He has chosen to show us grace. Why? Love!

God desperately and passionately loves you!

God could have left us to go our own way, but he simply loves us far too much for the story to end there. God loves us so much that he made a way for us to be redefined. And what we see through the pages of Scripture is the unfolding of the greatest rescue plan that eternity has ever seen, orchestrated by a loving Creator chasing after the people he loves.

The Creator and sustainer of the universe humbled himself (Phil. 2:6–7). God stepped off his throne, stepped out of eternity and into the bounds of time. He condescended himself, coming to earth in the form of a peasant baby

> God chooses to see our potential. The Creator looks beyond our depravity, choosing to love us in spite of our rebellious ways.

who was dependent upon a human mother. He exchanged divine omniscience for a finite human brain. He exchanged omnipresence for human legs. Instead of sitting on his throne in heaven, where he could oversee hundreds of billions of galaxies all at one time, he limited himself to living in the small country town of Nazareth. God intentionally handicapped himself, deliberately subjecting himself to all the grief of this world that we had brought upon ourselves. Jesus fully experienced the human life, with all of its joys and pains, all of its ups and downs, all of its lures and hardships.

Jesus came to earth to seek us out and save us (Luke 19:10). Motivated by love, and in spite of our hostility toward God, Jesus made a way for us to be redefined (Rom. 5:8–10). God made a way for human beings to be declared righteous and be called friends of God (James 2:23). Everything between God and us is restored to how it was before sin entered the story. We can have friendship with God once again . . . Jesus is the way!

> Jesus said to him, "I am the way, and the truth, and the life. No one comes to the Father except through me." (John 14:6)

Every genuine follower of Jesus is redefined by God and undergoes a supernatural transformation. God performs this amazing transformation. It is a sort of spiritual heart surgery. God exchanges our old poisoned heart for a new heart (Eze. 36:26). We are made into a new creation. He gives us new desires and a new hunger for purity. God exchanges our old nature for a new one. We are no longer slaves to sin, but slaves to righteousness (Rom 6:18). This transformation causes a profound, intrinsic

> God changes our status. He completely overhauls how he looks at us. He redefines who we are!

change deep within the soul of the believer. The Bible refers to this experience as being *born again* (John 3:1–7; 1 Pet. 1:3, 22–23; and James 1:18).

The caterpillar undergoes a tremendous metamorphosis, which makes it into a new creature. Likewise, the followers of Jesus have also been completely transformed. The old has gone, the new has come. We are born again!

God changes our status. He completely overhauls how he looks at us. He redefines who we are! Followers of Jesus are completely absolved of all guilt, of all blame! The heavenly High Court has dismissed all charges and declares that you are *not guilty!*

This divine redefinition dramatically changes everything. It changes our access to God and changes the way he relates to us. We have been elevated to a new status in the kingdom of God.

We are guaranteed to have our prayers heard. We can freely engage with God again. We are in his entourage and he takes great joy in spending time with us. The Creator of the universe desperately loves you and wants you to enjoy that tremendous love everyday.

We are newly adopted by God, labeled as his children, promised a heavenly inheritance, and given a secure position in his family. We are granted permanent access to have intimate friendship with God and we are bestowed with his favor. The image of God in us, which was once corrupted, has been restored. We are no longer slaves to sin; we have been endowed with the full power of God.

If you are a follower of Jesus, this is how God redefines who you are. These are God's declarations about you!

The Epidemic

The Almighty God desires to have a vibrant and dynamic relationship of love with each person who professes faith in Jesus Christ. Tragically, too many Christians never truly experience this sort of amazing love relationship with God.

Why do so many believers miss out on the divine love affair that God longs to have with them? I believe the number one reason is because they seem to think that God sees and treats them the same way that Brianna does caterpillars. Many believers do not understand that they have been redefined!

Many believers seem to think that God is repulsed by them, or that he is merely tolerating them. Many Christians see themselves as guilty failures; therefore they feel like God must be mad at them. But nothing could be further from the truth!

Labels play an essential role in our lives. *Human beings will often only rise up to the "status" they believe they are supposed to rise up to.*

Oftentimes, human beings embrace the wrong labels—labels that can greatly limit their potential. In a 2009 article, Diana Nygard, an educational expert turned blogger, remarked that "outlook and attitude—toward self or another person—can make or break a person's success in life."[1] Nygard has long observed this element of humanity within academic settings. Issues of labeling and pigeonholing are very real.

Human beings are very much influenced by labels and the opinions of others. We often allow opinions to influence how we view ourselves. We allow other people's perspectives to determine how we pigeonhole ourselves.

The classic twentieth-century author C. S. Lewis stated it this way: "We are what we believe we are!"[2] With this in mind, it is essential that we carefully examine what we believe about ourselves. More importantly, we ought to examine what God says about us!

Pastor and author J. D. Greear says, "Satan's most effective weapon is to take our eyes off of what God has declared over us in the gospel."[3] Nothing would make the devil happier than Christians misunderstanding their status in God's eyes. The devil is happy when he sees Christians disregarding their rightful positions in the family of God. One of the greatest tragedies of the contemporary church is that many sincere believers are ignorant of the truths that God has declared over us! This is an epidemic, a cancerous plague destroying the lives of many people. This is devastating churches and fracturing families.

The Labels We Embrace

Oftentimes, human beings embrace the wrong labels—labels that can limit our potential, or worse. Several years ago, I saw this clearly illustrated on my first trip to India.

I have been to more than twenty countries around the globe, but India is like no other place I've ever been. Stray cattle wander everywhere; the air is filled with the aromas of curry and sandalwood; there's a dizzying number of street vendors bombarding every would-be shopper; the streets are lined with an abundance of trash and sewage; and the erratic driving styles of the people could horrify Stephen King. Never will I forget what I experienced there.

More than the vivid images and unique smells, I will never forget the daily hardships the people face. Historically, Indian society divided people into social groups (known as castes) and imposed very strict limitations on the lower castes. While the traditional caste system is not nearly as strong in urban settings as it once was, it still continues today throughout the rural parts of the country.

During my first visit, I had a heartbreaking conversation with a Dalit woman that will stay with me forever. The Dalits are the lowest caste of India, often referred to as the *untouchables*. This woman and the other Dalits of her region live in extreme poverty, and often endure severe persecution at the hands of both local police and members of the upper-caste communities. They are forced to work in horrific conditions and are paid such low wages that many could legally be considered slaves. In many parts of India, the Dalits are denied access to public services, land ownership rights, education, freedom of religion, free choice of employment, and equal treatment before the law. In some rural parts of India, the sexual assault of Dalit women and young girls is extremely common. Often, crimes against the Dalits go unpunished.

The Dalit woman I met and spoke with had been terribly mistreated all her life. However, this wasn't the most outrageous aspect of our conversation. What I found to be absolutely shocking was the fact that she embraced this societal status. She genuinely believed that she was worthless and therefore deserving of this treatment. Speaking through our interpreter, she even told me that having a job or a source of income would literally be robbing from someone more deserving. She made it clear that she and her family would never seek to gain a higher status in this life, nor would they ever strive to better themselves in any fashion. They simply accepted this was their lot in life. She told me she had rejected Jesus Christ as a god in her life because she was offended by the idea of any god thinking she was valuable enough to die for.

She and her family could have moved to a more urban setting where the traditional caste system is far less rigid and where there are even some government provisions for the Dalits. But she and her entire family chose to live in accordance with the status pronounced upon them by their society. Many Dalit families wholeheartedly believe they deserve a life of abuse and oppression, and many more simply refuse to ever try to better themselves. Many Dalits seem incapable of changing their minds, while others are offended at the idea of breaking away from traditional Indian paradigms. Embracing these labels has been devastating to the Dalit people.

It may seem outrageous to us that anyone would choose to embrace the label of untouchable or the concept of worthlessness. It may be incomprehensible that people would choose to neglect certain freedoms or liberties. But this is not unique or native to India. In our Western societies, there are just as many people who embrace similar labeling. This is especially true in our contemporary churches.

Most Christians do not truly understand what Jesus Christ accomplished at the cross, nor do they understand their own transformation. They see themselves as untouchable—feeling dirty, tied to the ball and chain of guilt. Many more do not fully grasp the freedom they have in Christ, always feeling the burden of being the "perfect Christian" and constantly feeling like God is mad at them. Much like the Dalit people, many Christians have not embraced the right labels and therefore never experience the life that God longs for them to have. But we can change all of that!

God desires that we live abundant lives (John 10:10) and that we be fully satisfied in him (John 15:11; 17:13). He desires our minds and hearts to be continually captivated by his love for us.

God desires that we get rid of all guilt and shame within us. He wants us to walk with great confidence in him. Ultimately, God desires that we long for him, that we desire him above anything else, that we be fully content in him. And we were created for this. If we are not in love with God, we'll never be fully satisfied. We all have a God-shaped hole in our hearts. We are all desperate for a love relationship with God, but so many people don't realize this. The aching and emptiness in our hearts can only be filled and satisfied by the love of God.

The Westminster Shorter Catechism articulates it in this way, "Man's chief end is to glorify God, and to enjoy him forever."[4] Pastor and author John Piper puts it this way, "God is most glorified in us when we are most satisfied in him."[5] God calls us to enjoy him and be satisfied in him. God loves us and takes great pleasure when we experience his love. There is no wonder, then, why Satan would seek to keep us from that sort of amazing love relationship.

God wants you to be satisfied in him. He longs for you to experience his love. Misunderstanding how God has redefined you will be the number one obstacle to the magnificent plan God has for you.

If we continually embrace the wrong definitions of ourselves, we will continually limit our ability to enjoy intimacy with God— doomed to bear the weight of guilt. A Christian weighed down by guilt or shame can never fully enjoy God and can never fully glorify God.

It is impossible to have a quality friendship with God without understanding how we have been redefined.

Rightly understanding your divine redefinition will ignite reformation in your heart.

The Greatest Saboteur: Bad Thinking

One of the greatest obstacles you will ever face is your own self-image. When you embrace the wrong labels, you end up in trouble. This is what I call "bad thinking."

The church is filled with individuals who suffer from bad thinking. Flawed beliefs lead to thoughts that limit us. God cannot be glorified through your life if your bad thinking gets in the way. God desires that you break away from any thought patterns that have the potential to rob you of the abundant life he has ordained for you. *Bad thinking is sabotaging the church . . . and may be sabotaging your life, too.*

Many sincere Christians do not truly realize that God longs for intimacy. Some do not believe that they can be satisfied in God. Others do not trust his faithfulness. Many more do not

believe that the Holy Spirit has given them the
ability to overcome their sinful habits.

> The church is filled with individuals who suffer from bad thinking.

Can you imagine a monarch butterfly not
realizing that it has the ability to fly south for
the winter? How damaging would that be to
its well-being? It would die! Our churches are
filled with people who, metaphorically speaking, are not flying south for the winter; people
who aren't seeking that life-giving warmth in relationship with
God because they don't realize that they can.

Too many believers never fully enjoy friendship with God
because they don't know they have the opportunity to com-
mune with him. Many believers don't understand that their
purpose has been restored. Many fear that God is mad at them;
others feel as if God sees them as dirty or impure. Many believers rarely talk to God or they pray with such little confidence
because they feel like they have not earned the right to have
access to God.

God desires that we be faithful to his commands (John
14:15) and that sin have no power over us (Rom. 6:12), but
I have met lots of Christians who continually struggle with
habitual sin because they do not understand the power of God
to which they now have permanent access. Bad thinking is
wreaking havoc on many followers of Jesus.

For many years, I suffered from this sort of bad thinking. I
know firsthand the damage of allowing bad thinking to dom-
inate your mind and life. During both my teenage years and
young adult life, I lived far beneath God's greatest potential. I

was miserable. And as a result, my family and friends resisted listening to me about the Bible or the gospel message. One day I realized the reason behind their resistance. Why would they want my feeble, half-hearted, powerless brand of Christianity? I wasn't living much differently than they were. I wasn't involved in any of the "big sins," per se, but I was just as easily agitated, just as insecure, and just as frustrated with life as they were. I was riddled with guilt and shame. I never felt satisfied in God and often felt emotionally defeated.

But when I began to actually understand what God had exchanged in my life, everything changed! When I began to understand how God had redefined me, my love for God grew greater, and my hatred for sin grew, too.

When I started to grasp what God had actually done for me, my passions and desires changed. I began to realize the love relationship that God longed to have with me, but I had been missing out on. I had labeled myself as dirty and inadequate, but when I began to fully embrace the right labels—friend of God and child of God—I began to experience the abundant life that God desires for all his children. Understanding God's declarations about me in the gospel revolutionized my life.

> Strongholds are any ungodly beliefs that have a strong influence over how we make decisions.

We must choose to be aware of our beliefs about ourselves, about God, and about how God relates to us. If we are not keenly aware of these beliefs, we run the risk of developing strongholds. *Strongholds are any ungodly beliefs that have a strong influence over how we make decisions.* Strongholds will often hold us captive to destructive habits and disparaging insecurities. Any belief you might have that is contrary to the truth in the Word of God has the potential to become a stronghold, even if that ungodly belief is subconscious or seems relatively insignificant. It is essential that we allow God to kill the strongholds in our minds!

The Recipe for Bad Thinking

There are a variety of ingredients that may contribute to a sincere believer's being susceptible to bad thinking. All of those things can be combated with the right knowledge.

Far too many people, although they attend church and profess faith in Christ, lack decent biblical knowledge. They severely lack a strong foundation of biblical truth . . . and even fewer truly operate from a biblical worldview. William Douglas, the longtime United States Supreme Court Justice, once said, "The way to combat falsehoods is with truth."[6] If you suffer from bad thinking, the anecdote is to replace those false thoughts with truth. The best plan of attack is to saturate yourself with the truth from the Word of God.

Over the long haul of your Christian walk, your level of intimacy with God will only grow to the level of your understanding of his Word. Prayer and worship alone cannot bring about great freedom in your life, nor can any other element of Christian living. Prayer and worship and those sorts of spiritual disciplines are good, but if they are not coupled with the power of God's written Word, you will fall short of God's very best for your life. It is irrelevant how much anointing we might have on our lives or even how much self-control we've been able to demonstrate. Without deeply understanding the truth within God's Word, you are simply doomed to embrace the wrong labels and make wrong choices.

Jesus said, "If you abide in my word, you are truly my disciples, and you will know the truth, and the truth will set you free" (John 8:31–32). Jesus tells us exactly how to live a life of true freedom. We must know the truth and allow it to transform us.

If we are going to be victorious over sin, we need God's truth. King David wrote, "I have stored up your word in my heart, that I might not sin against you" (Ps. 119:11). Notice that he didn't merely memorize the words, but he stored them in his heart. This implies an intimate knowledge, a man deeply embracing the truths he found in Scripture.

Knowledge from the Word of God is essential. In Hosea 4:6, God says, "My people are destroyed for lack of knowledge." There are two key words in this verse. The first is "destroyed." The original Hebrew word for "destroyed" is *damah,* which can also mean "to be cut off," "to be undone," or "to be silenced." The second word of importance is "knowledge." This word comes from the original Hebrew word *da'ath.* The word "knowledge" does not mean mere information, but refers to understanding and perception.

In essence, this verse asserts that God's people are cut off because of a lack of understanding. What are they being cut off from? An intimate love relationship with the God of the universe! This is devastating to the life of the believer. The prophet Isaiah puts it this way, "Therefore my people are gone into captivity, because they have no knowledge" (Isa. 5:13 KJV).

The knowledge that Christians lack is specific to how God sees us, what God says about us, and the depth of God's power at work within us. Many believers seem to think that God views all of us as evil or dirty or wicked, or that he is easily disappointed in us. But that is simply not the case.

It is essential that we retrain the way we think. That we, as Christians, seek to comprehend the nature and extent of our divine redefinition. The depth of your understanding of what it means to be a new creation will make or break you!

That is why I wrote this book: to offer knowledge. My hope is to instruct as well as to inspire. Throughout the pages of this book we will examine a myriad of biblical concepts related to believers being divinely redefined, essential concepts such as the grace and the justice of God, imputation of righteousness, justification by faith, divine adoption, heavenly citizenship, and freedom in Christ. You may or may not already be aware of these doctrines; but by the end of this book, you will be intimately acquainted with them.

Having the right knowledge and embracing the right labels is the master key to reaching our greatest God-given potential and truly experiencing the love relationship with God for which we were created. Only by comprehending and embracing these precious doctrines can our hearts ever be fully satisfied in God.

Mind Renewal

To rid ourselves of bad thinking and strongholds, we must truly digest the Word of God. Truth from the Word of God is the cure for the cancerous plague damaging the church and our relationship with God. Truth is the antidote! God has a lot to say about what he has already exchanged in our lives; the Bible has a lot to say about how God views us and treats us and what he declares over us. As we examine those declarations, your life will be transformed.

The Apostle Paul tells us that true life transformation is the result of a renewed mind: "Be transformed by the renewing of your mind" (Rom. 12:2). Another Bible translation puts it this way: "Let God transform you into a new person by changing the way you think" (NLT). Changing your thinking is the avenue to real-life change. If you are ever going to be fully satisfied in God, you must renew your mind.

The world-renowned author Norman Vincent Peale wrote, "Change your thoughts and you change your world."[7] This is not about *doing* something right, but much more about *believing* something right. If you change the way you think to be in line with the truth in the Bible, then God will supernaturally transform your life.

Many Christians read the Bible like it's a fast food restaurant, grabbing a quick bite, just enough to satisfy the present gnawing hunger, and then quickly running off to the next task on the to-do list. In our contemporary, no-time-to-wait generation, we all want to be satisfied and nourished quickly. Many of us simply partake of just enough of God to satisfy our temporal needs, but never really take time to truly enjoy him, his Word, and his presence. We want the Bible on our terms, to meet our needs when we want them to be met. But I wonder . . . what if we took a different approach? What if we read the Bible . . . like it was a five-course meal?

What if we actually made time for God and his Word, and didn't just grab a quick bite? What if we paused to savor and enjoy each mouthful? What if we truly allowed the words from Scripture to be digested? What if we allowed the Word of God to get inside our souls? How would our churches be different? How might your understanding of God be different? How would you be different?

Let's do what the writer of the book of Hebrews encourages us to do: "Look to Jesus, the founder and perfecter of our faith" (Heb. 12:2). And in this you can be confident, assured that God will transform you. You can trust that he will develop you and mature you. The Apostle Paul reminds us "that he who began a good work in you will bring it to completion" (Phil. 1:6). God started this work in you. He will finish it!

Our part is to study the truth in the Bible and God's part is to supernaturally change our minds and lives. As we study how God has redefined us and as we embrace his truth, God will impart to us great wisdom and supernatural self-control.

As you renew your mind, you will soon notice that God is transforming you to be more like his Son, Jesus. Your love and appreciation for God will grow deeper than ever before. A change in your thought patterns will ignite a fire inside of you hotter than any campfire, greater than any California forest fire. You will hate your sin more and more each day, and you will begin to have the strength to overcome many of your old habitual sin patterns.

God desires that you live an abundant life, absolutely free from all guilt and shame, overflowing with the contagious joy that comes only from him. *God wants our lives to be branded by frequent victories over sin and marked by confidence in him!* This is the abundant life Christ promised . . . and you can have it! Abundant life begins with a thorough comprehension of the incredible transformation you have undergone, understanding that you have been redefined by God!

Take a journey with me. It's time to believe that you are a new creation. It's time to choose to view yourself as God sees you. It's time to retrain your brain!

Endnotes

1. Diana Nygard, "Negative Labels: How Do They Impact the Academic Success of a Student?" Yahoo! Voices, August 27, 2009, accessed February 9, 2013, http://voices.yahoo.com/negative-labels-they-impact-academic-success-4149237.html.

2. Marv Dumon, "C. S. Lewis Quotes," The Examiner, May 12, 2012, accessed February 9, 2013, http://www.examiner.com/article/c-s-lewis-quotes.

3. J. D. Greear, *Gospel: Recovering the Power that Made Christianity Revolutionary* (Nashville: B&H Books, 2011), 50.

4. "Westminster Shorter Catechism," Reformed.org, accessed August 23, 2013, http://www.reformed.org/documents/WSC.html.

5. John Piper, "God Is Most Glorified When We Are Satisfied in Him," DesiringGod.org, October 13, 2012, accessed February 9, 2013, http://www.desiringgod.org/resource-library/sermons/god-is-most-glorified-in-us-when-we-are-most-satisfied-in-him.

6. "William O. Douglas: The Mike Wallace Interview," Harry Ransom Center, May 11, 1958, accessed February 9, 2013, http://www.hrc.utexas.edu/multimedia/video/2008/wallace/douglas_william_t.html.

7. Norman Vincent Peale, *The Power of Positive Thinking* (Forest City, North Carolina: Fireside Books, 1952).

Heavenly Report Cards

As a child, I was an anomaly. Many young kids dislike school, but I loved it. I even loved homework. I guess I was sort of a nerd. At the end of each marking period, I'd typically bring home a report card consisting of mostly A's with just a few B's. My academic performance would often earn me praise from my parents.

One day, when I was in the fifth grade, something quite traumatic happened. The first quarter of the school year had just ended, so it was time to bring home a report card. I had my typical: mostly A's and a few B's. I was expecting the usual accolades. But this time it was different. My dad stood towering over me reading aloud the yellow half-sheet of paper that represented my academic success for the previous ten weeks. After he was done reading he paused. Finally he spoke, "Hmmm. . . . Did you see Amanda's report card?" I was puzzled. "Huh? What does she have to do with me?" And then, he told me. My sister Amanda, who was in the first grade, had done something I had never done. She brought home straight A's. *What? How? What the heck?* I thought. She was already daddy's favorite; why did she have to take my title as "brainiac," too? I was devastated!

A few days later, I was with my friend Ricky, who lived down the street from me. He had been a buddy of mine for many years, but we had never had any serious conversations. I told him about what happened and then he surprised me. He took a very serious tone (there's something special about a pair of ten-year old boys having a heart-to-heart talk while killing ants with a magnifying glass). Ricky told me about his older sister Anna who had always received better grades than he did. Ricky was a good kid, but his report cards often consisted of mostly C's with a few B's and D's sprinkled throughout.

Ricky believed that he could never live up to the standard that his mother had set for him, and he constantly felt like he needed to do more to earn her approval and affection. But his sister never seemed to have problems earning approval and affection from their mother. In several ways, he felt that Anna was the perfect kid.

Ricky then told me that he had imagined ripping up his own report card into tiny pieces, stealing Anna's report card, typing his name over her name, and present the report as his own. He felt like he couldn't earn those grades, so he imagined taking credit for what Anna was able to achieve. Ricky was convinced that if he could get credit for her work, then that would redefine how his mother viewed him and treated him. Maybe it would finally gain him the approval and affection he had so desperately been seeking.

Ricky's situation, and his hope of taking credit for Anna's work, gives us a glimpse into the gospel.

In essence, Jesus gives us credit for his achievements. When you become a follower of Jesus Christ, his perfect report card takes the place of your report card. Jesus takes his own report card and writes your name over his name.

Much like Ricky faced a standard that he could not live up to, we also face a particular standard that we cannot live up to. In the beginning, God set a standard for humanity. God expects righteousness! God expects human beings to live perfect, holy, righteous lives, in accordance with his commands. The problem is that none of us have ever lived up to that perfect standard.

Grades before Grace

Just like our grade school teachers who kept track of our performances during our school years, God also keeps records. God sees and tracks everything (Ps. 56:8; Dan. 7:9–10; Mal. 3:16–17; Rom. 2:15–16; Rev. 21:1–8). I guess you could say that each one of us has a "heavenly report card." Of course, the problem we face is our heavenly report cards reflect that we are evil and dirty and wicked.

God expects human beings to live perfect, holy, righteous lives, in accordance with his commands.

Before Jesus, we are found guilty!

Without Christ, the ledgers of heaven state that we are utter failures, that we are at odds with God. Before we believe and while sin still rules our lives, we are labeled as children of the devil (Matt. 13:36–43; John 8:44; 1 John 3:1–10). We deserve to be separated from God. We have earned the "wages of sin" (Rom. 6:23). It all started with Adam and Eve and has continued with each one of us:

> They have all turned aside; together they have become corrupt; there is no one who does good, not even one. (Ps. 14:3)

> For all have sinned and fall short of the glory of God. (Rom. 3:23)

Each and every person has freely chosen to do wrong. We have all betrayed God's moral inclinations. He created us to be like him and to experience his love, but we betrayed him and rejected him.

To have friendship with God and to enter into heaven, we must be perfect, as God is perfect, but none of us hit the mark. We can easily see the danger of our situation and our desperate need to be saved . . . we need a rescuer!

But even when presented with the facts, some people refuse to acknowledge the depth of our depravity. In many cases, this leads people to reject the notion that they need a rescuer. Some people claim that our sin isn't so bad. Some claim to be good because they have maintained a higher morality than other people, which I will certainly concede. But when it comes to how God views us, we are not compared to other people. God does not contrast human beings with other human beings; he contrasts human beings against himself. You might think you're naturally good compared to other people, but compared to God you're not good at all.

Humanity was originally created by God, in his own image, in a "state of innocency"[1] (Gen. 1:27, 31). But we allowed ourselves to be poisoned by sin. Our hearts, having been poisoned by sin, are more deceitful than anything else (Jer. 17:9). We bring destruction upon ourselves by following our own sinful cravings (James 1:14–15). We are in a state of hostility toward God (Rom. 8:7). Human beings are willing to exchange God's very best for lustful and corrupt things (Rom. 1:25). The Bible tells us that we are just as likely to change our own sinfulness as a leopard is to change his spots (Jer. 13:23). The great nineteenth-century preacher Charles Spurgeon penned this description of mankind: "You cannot slander human nature; it is worse than words can paint it."[2]

Our own ability to be good is tragically atrocious in comparison to God's ability to be good. We fail to meet his standard. We need to be made new.

If we must stand before God reliant upon our own heavenly report cards, then we're in serious trouble. The consequences of sin cannot be overstated! Eternal damnation will be far worse than you can possibly imagine.

Christ Steps In

Much like Ricky had imagined taking Anna's report card as his own, Jesus allows us to take his report card as our own. Jesus exchanges our record of wrongdoing with his record of perfect righteousness. Jesus takes on your report card, which reflects sin, and gives you credit for his report card, which reflects perfect righteousness. Jesus takes on the consequences that you and I deserve, and you get to enjoy the credit for his perfect achievements.

God demands that we have a record of perfect righteousness. Jesus makes a way for us to have our record of wrongdoing removed from us and makes a way for us to have his record of perfect righteousness transferred to us.

Of course, the exchange that Jesus offers is far greater than what my friend Ricky ever envisioned. In his scenario, his sister was not voluntarily offering up her report card. She wasn't ever looking to give away the credit for her hard-earned achievements. This is quite different from what Christ offers. Anna was not willing to volunteer for this exchange of error for perfection, but Jesus Christ, our rescuer, knowingly made an even more personal, permanent, soul-deep switch on our behalf.

Jesus gives us his own report card, and he writes your name over his own name. *But he doesn't use pencil or ink to write your name; he uses his own blood!*

Jesus came to earth and lived a perfect life. When faced with meeting God's perfect standard, Jesus passed the test with flying colors! Jesus was tempted with sin, just as we are. But unlike the rest of humanity, Jesus never sinned (Heb. 2:18; 4:15). His heart was never poisoned by sin. His heavenly report card reveals

> Jesus exchanges our record of wrongdoing with his record of perfect righteousness.

perfect righteousness! He lived a blameless life; he exhibited unmatched holiness.

Jesus earned a perfect heavenly report card. In the ledgers of heaven, Jesus is labeled as pure and righteous. And through faith in Jesus, his perfect report card can become our report card, and his righteousness can become our righteousness.

The Apostle Paul writes about Abraham's belief in God resulting in a label of righteousness (Rom. 4:3). Paul also tells us that "righteousness might be imputed" to all of us who believe (v. 11 KJV). This is the doctrine of the imputation of Christ's righteousness.

Imputation literally means to "charge" or to "credit." There is a double imputation that takes place. When we believe and trust in Christ, God charges our record of sin to Christ, sentencing Christ with the punishment of our sin and wickedness. God then also credits us with his very own righteousness, a righteousness that was present in Jesus Christ. Our sin is imputed to Jesus; his righteousness is imputed to us.

Amazingly, God allows us to take credit for Jesus' perfect actions, while allowing Jesus to take the blame for our sins. He suffered a horrific penalty for our sins. *This is the reason Christ came to earth!*

This double imputation is what the great sixteenth-century Reformer Martin Luther referred to as the "wonderful exchange":

> This is that mystery which is rich in divine grace to
> sinners: wherein by *a wonderful exchange* our sins
> are no longer ours but Christ's: and the righteousness

of Christ not Christ's but ours. He has emptied
himself of his righteousness that he might clothe us
with it and fill us with it: and he has taken our evils
upon himself that he might deliver us from them.[3]

This wonderful exchange is the very essence of the gospel message. We were all born at odds with God, enemies of God. But through faith he redefines how he sees you! God exchanges our lowly status for a greater status determined by this great imputation, the imputation of righteousness, from Christ to his followers.

God has fully erased your record of sin and replaced it with a record of righteousness. There is a new heavenly report card given to us! Without this wonderful exchange, God would have damned all of us to hell forever; but now, through Christ, we are declared righteous, and God is free to lavish his affection and favor upon us.

Through the work of Christ at the cross, we now have God's approval. Because of Jesus, we are no longer seen as sinful and wicked people, but rather as God's perfect children.

In order to make this wonderful exchange possible, Jesus chose to make an incredible sacrifice on our behalf.

The Wrath and Justice of God

Jesus suffered a brutal death. Why did Jesus endure this? To satisfy the wrath and justice of God.

God does not allow sin to go unpunished! It would compromise his integrity. Imagine a teacher who allowed a student to pass the class even though the records reflected that he had failed all the tests. That sort of teacher would violate the standards of the academic system. Or what about a modern day judge that simply refused to pass judgment on guilty criminals? Allowing a criminal to escape justice would only compromise the integrity and trustworthiness of the judicial system that the judge had sworn to uphold. In the same manner, God would violate his own character and his own moral law if he allowed sin to go unpunished. Allowing sin to go unpunished would simply be unjust. God is fiercely committed to seeing justice served. God loves justice (Isa. 61:8; Ps. 11:7; 33:5) and he has sworn to uphold justice (Job 34:11–12; Ps. 9:16).

The wrath of God must be satisfied. The justice of God must be served. God demands that sin be punished, but God hates to punish human beings. Because of God's great love for us, it deeply grieves his heart to condemn us (Ezek. 18:23, 32; 33:11). But God does not allow sin to go unaccounted for.

World-renowned author and professor of theology R. C. Sproul expounds by saying:

> God takes no delight in the death of the wicked,
> yet He most surely wills or decrees the death of the
> wicked. God's ultimate delight is in His own holiness
> and righteousness. When He judges the world, He
> delights in the vindication of His own righteousness
> and justice, yet He is not gleeful in a vindictive sense
> toward those who receive His judgment.[4]

Therefore, at some point in eternity past, motivated by his incredible love, God orchestrated the rescue plan, the plan by which sin could be punished, but sinners could be rescued. Jesus was sent to be the rescuer!

> For God did not send his Son into the world to
> condemn the world, but in order that the world might
> be saved through him. (John 3:17)

Through Jesus we are saved. Through faith in him we are now labeled as innocent and righteous.

In exchange, our sins have been imputed to Jesus. He took on our record of sin and failures. He had lived perfectly on this earth, but his record was marred, littered with our sins. He was charged with the guilt of our wrongdoings (Isa. 53:6, 10-11); our disobedience, acts of wickedness, and failures were all imputed to Christ. This is why he had to die a brutal death. Without his blood being spilled, sin could not be forgiven (Heb. 9:22).

Jesus did not go to the cross as an innocent man. As God incarnate (John 1:1, 14), Jesus never committed any sinful action whatsoever. Christ was morally upright, he had been fully innocent all his life, but at the cross he was declared to be sin (2 Cor. 5:21). This was the declaration upon him. Jesus lived a perfect life (1 Pet. 2:22), but he was charged with our sin, declared guilty, and severely punished!

Through the death of Christ on the cross, the wrath of God is satisfied and the justice of God is served.

Jesus: The Ultimate Stunt Man

A few years ago, I read a memorable account by actor Kevin Bacon. He was talking about the first time his young son saw the movie *Footloose*. "Hey Dad," Bacon recounted from the conversation with his son, "You know that thing where you swing from the rafters? That was really cool. How did you do that?" Bacon responded by telling his son about the film's stunt man. Bacon's son asked, "What's a stunt man?" Bacon's response to his son was something like, "Someone who steps in my place, dresses like me, and then does the things I can't do."

A little while later Bacon's son asked, "Hey Dad, you know that thing in the movie where you spin around on that gym bar and land on your feet? That was cool, too. How did you do that one?" Bacon again responded by explaining the movie magic of stunt doubles, this time referring to the gymnastics double that had been hired to play those specific parts of the film. Bacon vividly recounted the very confused look on his son's face, the contemplative silence, and then the awkward question that followed: "Well, Dad, what did you do?" Bacon's response to his son: "I got all the glory!" That's the gospel in a nutshell. Christ does all the work, and we get to take credit for it.

Through this wonderful exchange, Jesus rescues human beings. Everything Jesus did while he was here on earth was aimed at fulfilling this mission. He was our substitution. Jesus was the ultimate stunt man!

> No one takes [my life] from me, but I lay it down of my own accord. I have authority to lay it down, and I have authority to take it up again. (John 10:18)

> For Christ also suffered once for sins, the righteous for the unrighteous, that he might bring us to God,

> being put to death in the flesh but made alive in the
> spirit. (1 Pet. 3:18)

The wrath of God has already fallen upon Jesus Christ. Jesus stood in our place, taking the penalty that we deserved. *In his magnificent love for us, God made a way for us to receive forgiveness while still having his justice served. This was the genius of the cross!*

Jesus was our stand-in; Jesus was the ultimate stunt man!

Endnotes

1. "Westminster Confession of Faith," Reformed.org, accessed January 1, 2014, http://www.reformed.org/documents/wcf_with_proofs.

2. Charles Spurgeon, *The Salt Cellars, Volume Two* (London: Passmore and Alabaster; 1889), 8.

3. Martin Luther, quoted in J. I. Packer and Mark Dever, *In My Place Condemned He Stood* (Wheaton, Illinois: Crossway, 2008), 85.

4. R. C. Sproul, *Essential Truths of the Christian Faith* (Wheaton, Illinois: Tyndale House, 1998), 72.

Chapter 3

Air Force One

Not too long ago, I learned a very valuable biblical lesson about status from a movie starring one of my favorite actors, Harrison Ford. He is most famous for his roles as Indiana Jones, Han Solo, and CIA operative Jack Ryan. He was stellar in the 1985 classic film *Witness*, and even better as Dr. Kimble in the movie remake of the 1960s television series, *The Fugitive*. But as good as these flicks were, my favorite Harrison Ford movie is *Air Force One*.

In the 1997 box office hit, Harrison Ford's character, James Marshall, is the President of the United States. The movie gets its title from the call sign "Air Force One," which air traffic control assigns to any aircraft carrying the President. The very same aircraft, if the President is not on board, is assigned a different call sign.

In the movie, President Marshall is flying home to the United States with his family and his usual entourage after making a stirring anti-terrorism speech in Moscow. During the flight, a small band of militants hijack the plane and take hostages, including the President's wife and daughter. President Marshall, a former military hero, kills the terrorists one by one and eventually takes back the plane.

During the final few minutes of the film, the President is faced with another dilemma. *Air Force One* has become too damaged to fly and is quickly losing altitude. The hostages and crew are forced to unload the plane. A nearby Air Force cargo plane, *Liberty 24*, is dispatched to rescue them. In typical Hollywood melodramatic fashion, the survivors barely escape. They use a zip line to transport themselves from one plane to the other. At the end of the scene, after all the survivors are successfully transferred, the pilot of the small cargo plane makes an outstanding proclamation over the radio waves.

Before I highlight the pilot's profound statement, it is important to remember that *Air Force One* is not the actual name of the plane itself. *Air Force One* is a prominent symbol of the American presidency, its honor, and its power. As soon as the President steps on board any such aircraft, it is instantly entitled to all the rights, protections, provisions, and power that go along with the office of the presidency. An entire fleet of Air Force fighter jets are ready to protect this plane. It is the most famous and most photographed aircraft in the world. It is the most fiercely honored and highly maintained.

In that final scene of the film, when the pilot of the small cargo plane, *Liberty 24*, comes over the radio and makes his climactic statement, the entire President's staff back at the White House erupts with cheers of joy: "*Liberty 24* is changing call signs. *Liberty 24* is now *Air Force One*!" he said firmly. This declaration signaled that the President of the United States was safely on board the new aircraft. That small plane immediately inherited all the rights and all the provisions and all the protections that had been assigned to the plane the President had previously been on. *Liberty 24*, declared *Air Force One*, instantly rose to a new status. A revered status.

Regardless of the performance of that small plane, it was instantly designated the most important plane in the sky, entitled to guardianship. Did this small plane earn these rights and benefits, this new status? No; of course not! But the President stepped on board. That's all it took.

The spiritual parallels are obvious. As soon as our *spiritual president* stepped on board our lives, *we were instantly elevated to a new status.* No matter your previous quality, the very moment you placed your hope and faith in Jesus Christ, God exchanged the call sign of your life. This is an essential element of being redefined. This declaration is pronounced upon you through faith in Christ. Being redefined gives you a new status in God's eyes and guarantees you certain liberties. The Bible is clear that you have been elevated to a status far higher than anything you could have ever achieved on your own.

Embracing Your Divine Status

You have a choice to make. You can embrace whatever status has been pronounced upon you by others or the status that God has pronounced upon you. It is imperative that you embrace the right status and the right labels.

God says you are righteous!

I have heard so many believers respond by saying, "But I don't feel righteous." Well, therein is the problem. You must choose to embrace God's proclamation upon you more than you choose to believe your own emotions and feelings. Martin Luther once wrote: "You should not believe your conscience and your feelings more than the Word which the Lord, who receives sinners, preaches to you."[1]

Choosing to be governed by truth instead of your own feelings is certainly a tough task. Most people are as comfortable with embracing this discipline as the Amish are with embracing technology. But no matter how impossible the task may seem, it is vital to embrace God's truths more than your own emotions. *You must retrain your brain!*

You have been given a divine status. Now, when I speak of a divine status, I am not claiming that we are divine. What I am asserting is that we have a new status pronounced upon us that comes from the Divine One. It is God who performs the exchange. He exchanges our status as enemies with a new status: child of God.

The righteousness declared on our behalf is divine righteousness. The Apostle Paul spoke of this powerful declaration in his second letter to the Corinthian church:

Therefore, if anyone *is* in Christ, *he is* a
new creation; old things have passed away;
behold, all things have become new. Now
all things *are* of God, who has reconciled
us to Himself through Jesus Christ, and has given us
the ministry of reconciliation, that is, that God was in
Christ reconciling the world to Himself, not imputing
their trespasses to them, and has committed to us the
word of reconciliation.

> God says you
> are righteous!

Now then, we are ambassadors for Christ, as
though God were pleading through us: we implore
you on Christ's behalf, be reconciled to God. For He
made Him who knew no sin *to be* sin for us, *that we
might become the righteousness of God in Him.* (2 Cor.
5:17–21 NKJV, final emphasis mine)

This is absolutely one of my favorite passages in all of Scripture.
If you are in Christ, then you are a new creature. It is as if the
Apostle Paul is saying to you that you are like the monarch
butterfly. In God's eyes, you have been fully transformed. You
are brand new to him. You are gorgeous to him. The old nature
is gone. The new has come.

Paul tells us that God reconciled himself to us through
Christ. Reconcile comes from the Greek word *katallassō* which
literally means "to change or exchange."[2] God exchanged what
we were, depraved sinners, for what he intended us to be, righteous children of the King.

Notice this passage does not imply that we are merely a
fixed-up version of our old selves. No! Paul makes it clear the

"old self" is completely gone. There is a "new self" that has been born. Paul is talking about the wonderful, divine exchange. You have been completely redefined.

The sincere follower of Christ is no longer the same person. The nature and core of the believer are radically changed. The old person had a long record of sins and failures. This new person has a completely clean slate:

> All this is from God, who through Christ
> reconciled us to himself and gave us the ministry of
> reconciliation; that is, in Christ God was reconciling
> the world to himself, not counting their trespasses
> against them, and entrusting to us the message of
> reconciliation. (2 Cor. 5:18–19)

By being transformed into this new person, you have been given a fresh start. God no longer keeps a record of your sins or mistakes. He no longer holds your past transgressions against you. He approves of you and he gives you the opportunity to be his representative.

So, why do we continually remind ourselves of our pasts?

> Remember not the former things,
>   nor consider the things of old.
> Behold, I am doing a new thing;
>   now it springs forth, do you not perceive it?
> I will make a way in the wilderness
>   and rivers in the desert. . . .
>
> I, I am he
>   who blots out your transgressions for my own sake,

and I will not remember your sins.
(Isa. 43:18–19, 25)

And no longer shall each one teach his neighbor
and each his brother, saying, "Know the LORD," for
they shall all know me, from the least of them to the
greatest, declares the LORD. For I will forgive their
iniquity, and I will remember their sin no more.
(Jer. 31:34)

And he who was seated on the throne said, "Behold,
I am making all things new." Also he said, "Write this
down, for these words are trustworthy and true."
(Rev. 21:5)

The old person died at the cross with Christ. The new person
was raised with Christ. You are a new person—newly transformed—brought to life with Christ on that very first Easter
morning. As such, God no longer sees you as the caterpillar.
Instead, he chooses to see you as the beautiful monarch butterfly. You are no longer like *Liberty 24*, but *Air Force One*. You
have been elevated to a new status. You have been redefined!

Later in 2 Corinthians chapter 5, the Apostle Paul declares
that God has bestowed upon us the privilege of telling others
about the exchange: "[God] has given us the ministry of reconciliation. . . . Now then, we are ambassadors for Christ, as
though God were pleading through us" (vv. 18, 20 NKJV). We
are called to be God's ambassadors. God desires that we be the
instruments that he uses to rescue and redefine others. God
has written our story. Now we get to be a part of the story he

> God chooses to see you as blameless, morally upright, and perfectly clean.

is writing in the lives of the other people. Wow! What an honor!

The last portion of this passage, verse 21, is my favorite verse in the Bible: "For He made Him who knew no sin *to be* sin for us, *that we might become the righteousness of God in Him*" (final emphasis mine). We have been declared the "righteousness of God." God the Father stood before all of heaven to proclaim that when he looks at anyone in Christ, *he shall see them as just as righteous as he sees his own Son!* God says we are now right with him.

The Word of God is clear: God no longer views you as a depraved sinner. Instead, God chooses to see you as blameless, morally upright, and perfectly clean. Your status is righteous!

You have been labeled as innocent. Your faith in Christ has allowed you to have righteousness imputed to your record (Gal. 3:6-9). In the ledgers of heaven, you have gone from being an immoral sinner to being a righteous child of the King. And Jesus is your source for righteousness!

> And because of him you are in Christ Jesus, who became to us wisdom from God, righteousness and sanctification and redemption. (1 Cor. 1:30)

What Exactly Is Righteousness?

Up to this point, we have established that God has imputed his own righteousness to you. But what does it really mean to be labeled righteous?

The word *righteous* means "morally upright, without guilt or sin, to be in right standing." The word *righteousness* means "adhering to moral principles, a place or standing of the justification you have achieved at the highest level of standards possible."[3] Therefore, to possess righteousness means that the possessor has achieved the "highest level of standards possible."

To possess righteousness is to be someone who has a track record or reputation of being moral or good—and this track record is the basis of how you deserve to be treated. It is how God will determine what to do with you—both in this life and throughout eternity.

The Apostle Paul declares that all sincere followers of Jesus are labeled with the righteousness of God. God chooses to view us as people who live the "right way."

You may say, "This just isn't right; I am not righteous and I don't deserve this. I don't feel righteous." Well, by yourself, that's correct. On your own, you're not righteous. If you rely on your own ability to do right things, you do not deserve anything except hell. But thank God that your record in the ledgers of heaven is not based on your own goodness or your own abilities, but based upon the work of Christ.

A Lesson I Learned from Donald Trump

A few years ago, I was flipping through the television channels when I came across a show about Donald Trump's New York Penthouse Suites. The real estate agent took the elevator to the top floor and guided the cameraman through Trump's stunning multi-million dollar luxury condominium. She then proclaimed, "You can't get any higher up. You can't get anything better!"

That is how we are in the kingdom of God! Once you are born again, God proclaims that you are as high as you can get. You are the "best condo in town." This does not mean you have reached some hyper-spiritual sinless state of perfection where you can never do anything wrong. Certainly, our battle against sin is still very real and present, even after salvation. *However, this does mean that God's covenant with you is predicated on the fact that you have been proclaimed an individual that possesses the same righteousness that God himself possesses. You are in right standing with the King of kings.*

You were previously a disgusting sinner, but in one instance that radically changed! You now have this new divine status pronounced upon you. Your status doesn't change based on your behavior. You are declared righteous no matter how much or how little you sin.

God certainly desires for you to avoid sin—and he has empowered you with the Holy Spirit so that you might overcome sinful temptations—but whether you defeat sin or not has no bearing on your status in God's eyes. Your righteousness has been settled. You are now fighting against sin from a position of victory, not fighting to gain a position of victory.

You are the righteousness of God!

You are already declared to be as righteous as you are ever going to be. You can't become more righteous than what you've already been given. It would be like someone proclaiming that a monarch butterfly should become more like a butterfly; or if someone were to tell the crew of *Air Force One* to work harder so that they might achieve a higher status; or if some-one told the inhabitants of Donald Trump's suite to try and get to a higher floor. Your status is settled. You can't get any higher in God's eyes. You cannot ever become more "righteous" than what you already are.

> Our level of righteousness is predicated upon the life and death of Jesus; not predicated upon our works.

You can however choose to live in accordance with the righteousness already imputed to you. Previously, before faith in Christ, we were slaves to sin. We had no choice but to sin. But sin is no longer our master (Rom. 6:14). Now, by the grace of God, we are free to live righteously. God invites us to live righteously.

It is a noble thing to live like Jesus, to seek to overcome sin. Certainly we can become more like Christ in our habits and our choices, and we can mature in our faith. We can live out our righteousness more and more each day. But it is extremely important to make the distinction that living righteously does not cause you to be viewed as more righteous in God's eyes; and living unrighteously does not cause you to be viewed as less righteous in the sight of God. No matter our behavior, we cannot ever become more "righteous."

We cannot receive or attain a greater "right standing." God exchanged your old status. Our salvation is predicated upon our level of righteousness, and our level of righteousness is predicated upon the life and death of Jesus; not predicated upon our works.

Why is it so important to make this distinction? Because whenever we choose to believe our status in God's eyes is about our own behavior or performance, we often kick into *work mode*. Instead of truly enjoying God, we begin striving to impress him. Instead of seeing God as our loving daddy, we subconsciously begin to think of him as a demanding employer.

Instead of running to God in our moments of failure and insecurity, allowing his love and grace to comfort us, we feel this need to *fix* ourselves before we approach God—which, of course, is absolutely impossible.

When we believe our status is dependent upon our performance, we naturally stop delighting in the goodness of God; we're too busy to enjoy God because we are more concerned with measuring up to his standards.

If you do not understand that you are righteous, your spiritual development will be stunted. Not embracing your divine status will cause you to think less of yourself and limit your confidence in your ability to approach God.

Misunderstanding your status will cause you to embrace many of the wrong labels pronounced upon you by others, which will eventually cause you to make bad decisions. Not understanding how God sees you will greatly affect how often you pray and how you worship.

Preferred Status

I used to work for a Christian non-profit organization that required a lot of travel. I was typically in a different city each week. When you fly as often as I did, you earn preferred status with airlines. As a frequent flier with preferred status, you get certain perks.

I remember on one occasion I was traveling with a few colleagues who had not yet earned preferred status. We were checking luggage. John, one of my colleagues, was prepared to pay the checked luggage fee, but the airline employee never asked for his credit card. She just checked the luggage for him, gave us our boarding passes, and sent us on our way. A few minutes later John realized that, since he was with me, he did not have to pay the fee. One of the perks of having preferred status is free checked baggage. Typically airlines allow an entire party to enjoy this perk if even one person in the party has preferred status.

After we got our boarding passes, we headed toward the secured area. As we approached the security line, which was quite long, John grumbled, "Ugh, I hate waiting in these lines!" I responded with a chuckle, "What are you talking about dude? We're not going to wait in that line." He seemed confused. I reminded him that one of the best perks of having preferred status is the fact that you often get to skip the long lines at certain airports. Oftentimes, airports have a separate security line for preferred travelers. Very few things in life can make an adult man smile faster than realizing he doesn't have to wait in the long TSA line.

My friends had the opportunity to enjoy all of the perks of having preferred status. John had not earned the perks on his own, but he was suddenly entitled to enjoy them. My status was imputed to my colleagues on that trip. I had earned the status, and it was credited to them, as if they themselves had earned it. The only requirement was that they be with me. The spiritual parallels are obvious.

We are with Jesus. We're in his entourage. Therefore, we are imputed with his status. And we get to enjoy all the benefits that he has earned. We have not done anything to deserve the access to God that we now have, but we are entitled to enjoy it because of Jesus.

Now, can you imagine if one of my friends refused to accept the perks because he did not feel worthy? What if John, feeling like it was not right or fair, chose to go at it on his own? He would miss out on the benefits that he could rightly enjoy with my status being imputed to him.

There are loads of sincere Christians who have access to God and his benefits but simply refuse to embrace the status that Jesus has allowed to be imputed to them. If you do not embrace your divine status of righteousness, then you will forever (subconsciously) seek to "earn" or "achieve" some status with God, which will be a tremendous emotional burden and will only be met with failure. If we embrace what Jesus has already offered, we can enjoy all the benefits that he wants to give us. We cannot achieve any status with God on our own, but Jesus achieved it for us.

We Have Access to God

Several years ago while serving in youth ministry in San Diego, I lived on Coronado Island, just a few blocks away from one of the most beautiful beaches in Southern California. One day, my friend Josh invited me to play racquetball on the naval base on the northern half of the island. Josh was six inches taller than me, weighed at least fifty pounds less, and was a far superior athlete—but I still obliged. Other than my ego being bruised a bit, my embarrassment was an incredible comic relief for both of us. But what I happen to remember the most from that day is the ease with which we entered the military base.

On any previous occasion where I had gone onto a military base I had to get out of the car, check in, and get permission to go beyond the entrance. It was typically a lengthy (and somewhat nerve-wracking) process. But the morning I went with Josh was different. When we arrived at the main gate, a burly sergeant just waved us through without hesitation. Josh simply flashed an identification badge and through we went. He had free access to the naval base and his access was freely imputed to me. His right to be there instantly transferred to me as well.

The Holy Spirit instantly reminded me of my relationship with God. With Christ I have been freely given access to God the Father. This entitlement is one of the greatest benefits of being declared righteous.

My friendship with Josh gave me free access to that military base that day; likewise, my friendship with Jesus Christ enables me to walk freely and confidently into the presence of the Lord. I'm with Jesus. His rights and his access to the Father have been imputed to me. As long as I'm friends with Jesus, I'm all good! Jesus said these precious words:

> No longer do I call you servants, for the servant does not know what his master is doing; but I have called you friends, for all that I have heard from my Father I have made known to you. (John 15:15)

My pastor once told me that as his kids grew up, they had absolutely free access to enter into his office at any time. Regardless of who was in there, they could simply barge in. No permission needed; no announcement expected. He told me that there were occasion when they'd interrupt an important meeting just to say, "I love you, Daddy."

Good parents give their children total access, not because of something the children have done to deserve it, but simply because they are their children. In the same way, we have total access to God. We are his children. At any time of the day, we can thank him and pray to him. At any time of the day, we can bring our petitions before him. And at any time of the day, on demand, we can interrupt him with absolute confidence that he will stop to pay attention to us.

> Christ Jesus our Lord, in whom we have boldness
> and access with confidence through our faith in him.
> (Eph. 3:11–12)

> Since then we have a great high priest who has passed
> through the heavens, Jesus, the Son of God. . . . Let us
> then with confidence draw near to the throne of
> grace, that we may receive mercy and find grace to
> help in time of need. (Heb. 4:14, 16)

Our access to God is not based on our merits. It is based on Jesus. He lived the sinless life and died the brutal death that purchased our right to access God. The death of Jesus brought us forgiveness (Lev. 22:21; Heb. 9:22). But his death didn't stop there. He purchased more than that for us. The Bible makes it clear that we can have the utmost confidence to enter even in the holy place (Heb. 10:19). We have the legal right to enter God's presence

> Our access to God is not based on our merits. It is based on Jesus.

because the blood of Jesus was the payment for the establishment for the better covenant (Heb. 7:22).

We have permanent access to the fullness of God. We can still walk with absolute confidence knowing that God will always meet us in our time of need. Author and longtime missionary to India, Wesley Duewel, made this awesome statement:

> The greatest privilege God gives to you is the freedom to approach Him at any time. You are not only authorized to speak to Him; you are invited. You are not only permitted; you are expected. God waits for you to communicate with Him. You have instant, direct access to God. God loves mankind so much, and in a very special sense His children, that He has made Himself available to you at all times.[4]

We can stand before him with confidence. He loves us and invites us to approach him. Our access to God is never negated or discounted. We never need to feel guilty or embarrassed to approach God. *Never!*

What Does God See?

"What does God see when he looks at me?" This is an important question to ask. Your answer might be able to help you diagnose whether or not you have been suffering from bad thinking.

I think one major reason believers often neglect their access to God is because they feel unworthy. They do not understand what God sees when he looks at us.

When God looks at his children, he sees us as being *in* Christ. We inherit all the favor that Jesus earned. Jesus is an heir of God; therefore, we are heirs of God (Rom. 8:17). God approves of Jesus; therefore, God approves of us. God has lavished his daddy-love on Christ, so we can be confident that he will also lavish his daddy-love on us. When God looks at us, he does not look at us on our own, because we are in Christ. God sees us through the lens of the righteousness of Christ:

> For you died, and your life is hidden with Christ in
> God. When Christ who is your life appears, then you
> also will appear with him in glory. (Col. 3:3–4)

When God the Father looks at the record of any genuine Christian, he sees nothing but absolute perfection, the same perfection he saw in Christ. Through faith in Jesus we have a fresh start. The slate is wiped clean:

> "Come now, let us reason together, says the LORD:
>   though your sins are like scarlet,
>   they shall be as white as snow;
>   though they are red like crimson,
>   they shall become like wool." (Isa. 1:18)

Motivated by his incredible love for us, Jesus died for us so that we might be declared "holy" and be made "without spot or wrinkle" (Eph. 5:25–27). If you have placed your full faith in Jesus, then you have his perfect righteousness imputed to you.

Many sincere believers inwardly battle emotions of feeling constantly weighed down by the ball and chain of guilt because they have not embraced these truths. In Christ, you never have any reason to feel guilty. You never have to embrace shame. If you are in the category of people constantly feeling guilty, often feeling like you don't measure up or that you're not good enough, it is time for a change. I would encourage you to memorize some of the Bible verses I have outlined here and spend substantial time in personal prayer, reflecting on your own beliefs (possible strongholds) and meditating upon these truths from God's Word.

Guilt and shame cause us to sell ourselves short—to settle for less than God's very best. People who feel guilty will succumb to sinful temptations more often than those people who have embraced forgiveness. Guilt is one of the greatest obstacles. But God declares that you do not have to feel guilty. You never need to feel ashamed or discouraged. The Apostle Paul wrote these powerful words: "There is therefore now no condemnation for those who are in Christ Jesus" (Rom. 8:1). One contemporary paraphrase puts it this way:

> No condemnation now hangs over the head of those
> who are "in" Jesus Christ. For the new spiritual
> principle of life "in" Christ lifts me out of the old
> vicious circle of sin and death. (vv. 1–2 PHILLIPS)

God declares that nothing is hanging over our heads!

Many people tend to be very critical of themselves. We often demand, of ourselves, that we actually *do* something to earn our status. But God does not deal with us according to what we deserve, nor is his approach toward us ever in accordance with what we feel about ourselves. We are recipients of an undeserved forgiveness; an amazing grace! God says we are no longer condemned. The slate is wiped clean!

We have been declared righteous! There is nothing that you or I can do to merit or earn this amazing grace!

Jesus made it possible for us to have the clean record. Guilt and shame are truly eradicated from our lives when we see ourselves as clean and righteous:

> For God has done what the law, weakened by the flesh, could not do. By sending his own Son in the likeness of sinful flesh and for sin, he condemned sin in the flesh, in order that the righteous requirement of the law might be fulfilled in us. (Rom. 8:3–4)

> He has delivered us from the domain of darkness and transferred us to the kingdom of his beloved Son, in whom we have redemption, the forgiveness of sins. (Col. 1:13–14)

God forgives you of all your sin and declares you righteous. Therefore, you can stand before him with confidence that he does not see any fault in you. When you were redefined by God, the perfect report card that Jesus earned became your report card.

You are the righteousness of God!

So, what must we do in order to obtain this outstanding righteousness? How do we become a member of his family? How do we ensure that we have been redefined?

We will thoroughly unpack the answer to these questions in the next chapter. The answer is really simple, and it's something you may have already done. *Simply believe!*

Endnotes

1. Paul Althaus, *The Theology of Martin Luther* (Minneapolis: Fortress Press, 1966), 59.

2. Sowing Circle, Inc., *Blue Letter Bible*, "Greek Lexicon::G2644 (KJV)," accessed August 11, 2011, http://www.blueletterbible.org/lang/lexicon/lexicon.cfm?Strongs=G2644&t=KJV.

3. Dictionary.com, LLC, "Righteous | Define Righteous at Dictionary.com," accessed February 9, 2013, from http://dictionary.reference.com/browse/righteous?s=t.

4. Wesley L. Duewel, *Touch the World through Prayer* (Grand Rapids: Zondervan, 1986), 21.

Chapter 4

Belief, Not Behavior

The basis for our rescue is belief. Author and Yale University professor William Lyon Phelps said it best with these simple words: "The Gateway to Christianity is not through an intricate labyrinth of dogma, but by a simple belief in the person of Christ."[1]

The most well-known Bible verse contains these words from Jesus, "Whosoever *believeth* in him should not perish" (John 3:16 KJV, emphasis mine). If you've been an attender of church for any length of time, you've heard these words, but still it appears that many of us find it hard to understand that simple *belief* allows us to obtain righteousness. Jesus later said these precious words, "Truly, truly, I say to you, whoever *believes* has eternal life" (John 6:47, emphasis mine).

> The Gateway
> to Christianity
> is not through
> an intricate
> labyrinth of
> dogma, but by
> a simple belief
> in the person of
> Christ.
>
> —William Lyon Phelps

In his letter to the Romans, the Apostle Paul presents the case for righteousness through belief . . . not behavior. He takes his readers down a path where he systematically explains how we are declared to be the righteousness of God: "For in it the righteousness of God is revealed from faith for faith" (Rom. 1:17).

Though the letter begins with these words, you would not know it contained good news by only reading the first few pages. Paul spends most of the first three chapters elaborating on human depravity. Paul explains why our heavenly report cards were utter failures. However, toward the end of the third chapter of Romans, his tone begins to change significantly. Paul's excitement grows as he explains the actions taken by God to reconcile us back to himself:

> But now the righteousness of God has been manifested apart from the law, although the Law and the Prophets bear witness to it—*the righteousness of God through faith in Jesus Christ for all who believe.* For there is no distinction: for all have sinned and fall short of the glory of God. (vv. 21–23, emphasis mine)

The first word here is "but." Oh, I love when there is a *but* in the Word of God. Yes, we were depraved. Yes, we were enemies of God. Yes, we were failures. Yes, we were total losers. Yes, we deserved to burn in hell forever . . . yes, yes, yes . . . *BUT* . . . you can still obtain righteousness! *Hallelujah!*

Paul is telling us about a form of righteousness that we can obtain that is "apart from the law." We can be labeled as righteous in God's eyes without having to be perfect in this life. Our righteousness comes from Christ. The Apostle clearly teaches us how to obtain this righteousness that is found "apart from the law." He writes that it is "through faith in Jesus Christ to all who believe."

> . . . the righteousness of God through faith in Jesus Christ for all who believe. For there is no distinction: for all have sinned and fall short of the glory of God, *and are justified by his grace as a gift, through the redemption that is in Christ Jesus,* whom God put forward as a propitiation by his blood, to be received by faith. This was to show God's righteousness, because in his divine forbearance he had passed over former sins. (vv. 22–25, emphasis mine)

We Are Justified by Faith

As an element of the imputation of righteousness, we have been declared fully innocent in the sight of God! Our sinful records are completely eradicated, fully expunged. This absolute eradication of our sinful record is known as "justification."

My pastor back in Philadelphia, Joe Focht, would often describe justification by saying, "justified means 'just-as-if' it never happened." To be justified is to have your sins fully erased; just as if you had never committed those sins in the first place. It's like going back in time and changing history.

We have all sinned and we have all earned the judgment that comes with that sin. But through faith in Christ we can be "justified freely by his grace" (Rom. 3:24 NIV). We are justified through faith! Jesus has chosen to forget your past sins and has wiped the record clean. With God your past never defines you. The salvific work of Christ defines you. (Justification is such an essential doctrine we will examine it in closer detail later in this book).

Imputation of righteousness and full justification happen through faith!

What Is Faith?

A pastor friend of mine recently Tweeted, "Faith in its simplest form is agreeing with God." While this is a rather elementary definition, it does give us insight into the pragmatics of faith. Do you agree with God? When God speaks through his Word, are you 100 percent convinced that it's true or do you doubt what he has said?

The word "faith" Paul uses in Romans 3 comes from the Greek word *pistis*, which literally means "to have a conviction of the truth" or "to have a true belief of something."[2] This is a simple state of mind that results in fervent trust. *Faith is a matter of choosing to genuinely and sincerely believe, not a matter of choosing to properly behave.* True faith is a belief that will result in people behaving differently, but the action of behavioral change itself is not faith.

Genuine faith in Christ can also be described as *personal trust* in Christ. Allow me to illustrate genuine faith. Right now, as you read this book, you are most likely sitting in a chair of some sort. You put your full body weight on that chair and trust that it will hold you up. And you chose to believe this *before* actually sitting down. You were convinced of the chair's ability in your mind. You then outwardly demonstrated your faith in the chair by then actually sitting in it. Essentially, this is faith. You believed. You were convinced.

> Faith is not a mere intellectual awareness of Christ, but rather a genuine trust in him and in his ability to save.

Genuine faith in God is no different. Your faith in Christ was a belief you chose to embrace, a conviction of truth in your mind. Having faith in God means you are fully convinced that the God of the Bible is real and you are willing to trust him—a confident knowledge, much like Job declared, "I know that my Redeemer lives" (Job 19:25).

Genuine faith in Christ saves. *At the precise moment that you placed your faith in Christ, you were transformed and God pronounced to all of heaven that you are his righteousness.* God the Father credited Christ's record of perfect obedience to your record. If you have chosen to genuinely believe in Christ, then God has forgiven you of all your sins and he has imputed to you the righteousness of God. Faith in Christ saves:

> *For by grace you have been saved through faith.* And this is not your own doing; it is the gift of God, not a result of works, so that no one may boast. (Eph. 2:8–9, emphasis mine).

Faith is not a mere intellectual awareness of Christ, but rather a genuine trust in him and in his ability to save. Are you fully persuaded and absolutely convinced that Jesus Christ is the only way? Do you sincerely believe that in your heart? Have you been willing to make that sort of confident profession? If so, then you are saved. It is by faith you are saved:

> Because, if you confess with your mouth that Jesus is Lord and believe in your heart that God raised him from the dead, you will be saved. For *with the heart one believes and is justified*, and with the mouth one confesses and is saved. For the Scripture says, "*Everyone who believes in him will not be put to shame.*" (Rom. 10:9–11, emphasis mine)

After conversion, many Christians experience radical lifestyle changes. The Holy Spirit dwells within the heart of the believer, helping him to withstand temptation. It is the Holy Spirit who causes us to love and crave God, and who causes us to want to be more like him. The Holy Spirit molds and empowers us to live Christ-honoring lifestyles. Our performance does not determine our salvation or even our status with God, but we as believers are still very much called to live as holy as possible, through the power of the Holy Spirit.

And It Was Credited to Him as Righteousness

The Apostle Paul continues to build an incredible case for righteousness by faith using the example of Abraham. In Romans 4:1–2 Paul says, "What then shall we say was gained by Abraham, our forefather according to the flesh? For if Abraham was justified by works, he has something to boast about." Here Paul explains that there was no one better than Abraham. If righteousness could be obtained by performance or being good, then Abraham would have something to brag about.

Abraham was great . . . but that didn't justify him. His good works got him nowhere. He was still a depraved sinner under the curse of iniquity, separated from God, and destined for hell—until he believed God.

In Romans 4:3, Paul explains why Abraham was declared righteous: *"Abraham believed God and it was credited to him as righteousness"* (emphasis mine). Notice that the verse does not say, "Abraham believed God and he tithed a little extra that week and it was credited to him as righteousness." Nope, it doesn't say that. And notice this passage does not say, "Abraham believed God and he stopped cussing and never watched an R-rated movie, so God credited to him righteousness." Nor does it say, "Abraham believed God and he fixed up his life and he got rid of all of his sin and it was credited to him as righteousness." Wrong again; that's not what the passage says. The Bible makes it very clear. Abraham was credited with righteousness because he *believed* God. No qualifiers!

The same applies to us today. If we believe God, it will be credited to us as righteousness. Faith generates this status, not behavior or performance; therefore, behavior cannot nullify this status. Our righteousness comes from faith and depends on faith (Phil. 3:9). Christians are always in right standing with God because we have his righteousness.

You are the righteousness of God in Christ! God has placed his stamp of approval of you. God does not use a Daily Tracking Poll to determine his approval rating of you. God the Father uses Christ's actions on the cross to determine his opinion of you. The fourth chapter of Romans ends with Paul making these remarks about Abraham:

> No distrust made him waver concerning the promise of God, but he grew strong in his faith as he gave glory to God, fully convinced that God was able to do what he had promised. *That is why his faith was "counted to him as righteousness."* But the words "it was counted to him" were not written for his sake alone, but for ours also. *It will be counted to us who believe in him who raised from the dead Jesus our Lord,* who was delivered up for our trespasses and raised for our justification. (vv. 20–25, emphasis mine)

The Apostle tells us that Abraham "did not waver through unbelief," but instead he was "fully persuaded." This is why he was declared righteous. This is the same "for us who believe in him." Ask yourself, "Do I waiver through unbelief?" Have you been fully persuaded that Christ is the only way?

Belief Effects Behavior

Several years ago, I noticed a car stopped on the side of the road as I drove toward a toll-bridge. I stopped alongside the car and yelled out my window, "Everything okay?"

The man yelled back, "I don't have any cash on me. They don't take credit cards. I'm going to have to turn around and find an ATM."

I responded, "Nah, don't do that. I'll take care of it for you. Just follow me!" The man was both shocked and elated that I made such an offer.

After our brief conversation, I rolled up my window and starting driving forward with the hope that the man would indeed trust me and actually follow me. At this point, the man was faced with a choice. He could choose to take me at my word, or he could choose not to believe me and try to do it on his own.

Some might say the man had to put some actions behind his belief. He couldn't just claim to believe me; he also had to follow me. Doesn't that involve actions? Isn't that more than just simple belief? Great questions!

The man did indeed show some actions. But it was not the actions that caused him to become a believer. The actions are the evidence of his belief. He became a believer at the very moment that he determined to trust my words. First, he chose to believe; afterward, his actions proved he had in fact believed me. His confidence in me influenced his behavior.

The man was going to take some sort of action anyway. He was either going to follow me because he believed me, or he was going to go at the problem on his own. It was at the precise moment that he chose to believe me that he could be credited as a believer . . . *before* he physically followed me! His actions would then be predicated on his beliefs. If the man had claimed to believe me and then never followed me, that would be the evidence that he lied to me—that he did not take me at my word. His lack of action would demonstrate a lack of genuine faith in the promise I made to him.

Jesus has made an offer to pay your debt. You simply need to choose to believe and take him at his word. But you cannot just believe in him. Many people believe that a man named

Jesus existed. That's not what I'm referring to. There's more to it than that. Do you truly believe him? Do you believe his Word? Or will you try to solve your sin problem on your own?

Again, some people would contend that we can't just verbally claim that we believe, but rather we must "follow" Jesus to be saved. Yes, indeed, Jesus does call us to follow him, but it's similar to how I invited that man on the side of the road to follow me. That man first needed to believe my words; otherwise, he would have never followed me.

The basis for following Jesus is simple belief in his words. When God calls us to follow him, he is basically saying that he wants us to have genuine belief in him; a belief that is so strong that we eventually choose to cling to him in our everyday lives, and it becomes evident to everyone by our actions, attitudes, and choices. Jesus invites us to believe him so firmly that we begin to live and love the way he did while he was here on earth. Jesus calls us to deeply trust his words, so much so that we begin to live in radical obedience to the commands of Scripture. But it all begins with simple belief.

> Jesus calls us to deeply trust his words, so much so that we begin to live in radical obedience to the commands of Scripture.

Your behavior does not make you righteous in the sight of God, but your belief will certainly influence your behavior, causing you to become more Christ-like.

Your actions will prove whether or not your initial belief was genuine. The overall direction of my life will show that I have indeed believed God. Of course, even after my belief, it is very possible (and highly likely) that I will have moments of great failure; moments that make it seem like I lack genuine belief in God. But even in those moments of failure, I do not lose my righteous standing. Even when I fail, I still possess the righteousness of God. Even when I sin, I am still deemed innocent and blameless and free of all guilt. I have the righteousness of God credited to my record, even when my lifestyle doesn't perfectly reflect it. I have believed God and it has been credited to me as righteousness.

With the confidence that I am labeled completely righteous at the very moment of my belief, I can walk and pray and worship without ever doubting that God loves me and invites me to approach him. Even when I blow it, even when I make stupid decisions, even when I sin, I still feel confident to come to him. No matter how much I have sinned or how little I have prayed, I never have to feel dirty or inadequate. I know that I can still boldly come to him (Eph. 3:12; Heb. 4:16), knowing that he will comfort me and minister to me.

God is All-In

Quite frankly, I rarely feel like I am a good Christian (and I'm not even sure how to define "*good Christian*" anyhow). I know myself all too well. I have often seen the pride and selfishness of my own heart. I have failed more times than I'd like to admit. But I am very confident, even in my moments of failure, that I can run to Jesus. I am confident that my Daddy God will have his arms wide open, ready to embrace me, to lavish his love on me!

God is "all-in" on me! He is fully committed to me. My folly does not change his opinion of me. My mistakes do not negate his commitment to me. Nothing can separate me from his unconditional love (Rom. 8:38-39). He will never leave me, nor forsake me (Heb. 13:5-6).

For as long as I continue to believe, my perfect righteousness remains intact and God remains committed to me. And how can I be sure that my belief will continue and remain? Well, because he promised to make sure of it. God is supernaturally working in the hearts and lives of all believers, causing us to continually trust him. It is not dependent upon my power to remain faithful, but on his power to keep me faithful.

If my belief were up to me, there is no chance that I'd ever stick with it. God is the one who gave me the ability to believe (John 6:28-29; Phil. 1:29). In fact, none of us would have ever believed if God had not first given us the ability to believe in him (John 6:44, 65). Jesus is the one who authors our faith and he is the one who makes our faith perfect so that we will continue believing (Heb. 12:2).

It is the will of God that every person who believes in Jesus be saved, and Jesus promised that any person who has ever believed will never be lost (John 6:37-40). Not one will slip through his fingers. No one can snatch us from his hand (John 10:28). God promises that he will "sustain you to the end, guiltless in the day of our Lord Jesus Christ" (1 Cor. 1:8). It is God who shields us so that we might receive salvation (1 Pet. 1:5). This is all dependent upon him and his unconditional commitment to me. He enables and causes me to believe. This is a supernatural and sovereign work of God. There are no words in any human language that could ever express how grateful I am that he has committed himself to me.

If my salvation were dependent upon my own ability to remain faithful to him, I would be in some serious trouble. But, I am now certain that I will remain faithful to him, and my belief will remain strong, not because of any ability in me of my own volition, but because he will continually give me the ability to believe and remain faithful.

It is all about God and his faithfulness.

Don't Miss Your "God Moments"

Many times, before I embraced my righteous standing, I missed out on so many moments of intimacy with God. I remember multiple instances when I entered a church filled with singing and worship, but since I had brought with me feelings of guilt and sin, I would refrain from participating in the worship. I'd sing aloud, so outwardly it'd appear as if I was totally engaged, but my inward mind and heart would not be. I'd repent of my sin but still feel unworthy to jump right into worship. I'd wait until I felt I had worked my way up to being "good enough," letting the first three or four songs go by, and maybe let my heart join in on the last song. But by that point I'd missed out on an incredible opportunity to worship. Does this scenario sound familiar?

Or what about missing out on prayer? I cannot tell you how many times I have neglected prayer because I felt unworthy to talk to God. I used to think that in order to have effective prayers, I must have been a really good Christian. I figured, "Oh man, I sinned a lot this week so my prayers won't be heard. I'm not good enough, so God won't listen." I may not have ever articulated my feelings in this way, but that's how I felt inside.

> Satan knows that if he can keep us from experiencing freedom through full access to God, then he can keep us from reaching our full potential.

The Apostle James tells us that the prayers of the righteous have great power (James 5:16). Well, that's us!

If you understand that you are declared righteous no matter what you do, you'll know that your prayers are always effective, no matter what. James tells us that when righteous people pray, their prayers have great influence. I can always be absolutely confident that God is listening. Understanding my righteous state completely revolutionized the way I prayed.

Before really embracing imputed righteousness, I often robbed myself of opportunities to connect with God because I felt ashamed. God does not want us to ever feel this way. God wants us to always run to him—no matter how we feel.

Satan would love to keep you from experiencing everything God has ordained. He would love to rob you of some great "God moments." He has already lost the war for our souls. But he won't stop trying to win smaller battles along the way. Satan knows that if he can keep us from experiencing freedom through full access to God, then he can keep us from reaching our full potential. But through the power of the Holy Spirit, we can be victorious.

God has ordained us to live abundant Spirit-led lives, overflowing with his love and life-transforming power. This is not to say that we won't face hard times. We are not absolved from living on this depraved and fallen planet; therefore, we can assume the pain of this sinful world will still affect us. But we do not need to face the ills and hardships of this world alone. Because of our confidence in God's commitment to us, we can be sure that he will be with us and guide us through difficulty. Paul wrote these words:

> More than that, we rejoice in our sufferings, knowing
> that suffering produces endurance, and endurance
> produces character, and character produces hope,
> and hope does not put us to shame, because God's
> love has been poured into our hearts through the
> Holy Spirit who has been given to us. (Rom. 5:3–5)

We will face tough situations, but we do not need to face them with the same sorrow or fear that unsaved people deal with. Rather, we can rejoice while we go through tough times because we know that God will be with us.

God comforts us in hard times and he makes our afflictions purposeful (2 Cor. 1:3-5). We know God will use difficult circumstances to develop our character and work all things for our good (Rom. 8:28). God will always be with us (Jos. 1:9; Matt. 28:20). God continually sustains us through all things (Psalm 54:4; 55:22).

God makes this available because he loves us. We can be confident that God will continually lavish his love and affection on us. How much does God love us? So much so, that while we were still his enemies, he chose to die for us. He chose to sacrifice himself for us, long before we ever considered doing anything for him:

> But God shows his love for us in that while we were
> still sinners, Christ died for us. Since, therefore, we
> have now been justified by his blood, much more
> shall we be saved by him from the wrath of God. For
> if while we were enemies we were reconciled to God
> by the death of his Son, much more, now that we are
> reconciled, shall we be saved by his life. (Rom. 5:8–10)

God loved us so much he chose to send his Son to die for us long before we ever considered loving him. If Christ was willing to show that sort of love while we were still his enemies, how much more will he demonstrate his love for us now that we are his friends?

We have the righteousness of God imputed to our records and we now have permanent access to God. Nothing we do will ever negate our righteous standing before God. He will sustain us and keep us.

All of this is from God through simple belief in Christ.

Endnotes

1. QuotationsBook.com, *Quotes About Belief* (Quotations Book, 2013), 20, eBook edition, http://books.google.com/books?id=-JOJU7J5NNMC&printsec=frontcover&dq=Quotes+About+Belief&hl=en&sa=X&ei=oS0pUcqNCJDy2gW8roCwBw&ved=0CDEQ6wEwAA.

2. Sowing Circle, Inc., *Blue Letter Bible*, "Greek Lexicon::G4102 (KJV)." accessed February 9, 2013, http://www.blueletterbible.org/lang/lexicon/lexicon.cfm?Strongs=G4102&t=KJV.

Chapter

Grace: License to Sin?

If you believe, then you are completely righteous in the sight of God. And there is nothing you could ever do that would change that. You didn't become righteous by being good, so you can't become unrighteous by being bad.

Oh, how I can hear the critics now, telling me that I have given a bunch of people a *license to sin*. I've been accused of making the gospel and the Christian life "too easy." I even once had someone accuse me of offering "greasy grace" (still not sure exactly what that means). Many people are nervous about proclaiming a raw, unbridled message of grace, because grace comes with a hint of scandal. But I am not afraid to boldly preach the grace that is clearly offered by God in the Bible.

As for those people who might want to accuse me of having made grace too easy? To them I say, well, I am not the one who made access to God too easy. The credit belongs solely to the Savior. Jesus openly stated, "My yoke is easy, and my burden is light" (Matt. 11:30).

It is important to understand the imagery Jesus uses here. Literally speaking, a yoke is a curved wooden beam used in farming. It is fitted around the necks of two oxen for the purpose of securing them together, so that they can work together in pulling a plow and performing other farming tasks.

The term "yoke" is used throughout the Bible metaphorically. It was often used in the first century by religious leaders to refer to how they believed a person could be bound to God. Basically, a particular yoke dictated what human beings must do in order to be accepted by God. The Pharisees imposed many rules and regulations on the Jews. It was virtually impossible to uphold all of them. This led to many people feeling guilty and rejected by God. Others resented God because he seemed too hard to please. The yoke of the Pharisees was oppressive, emotionally taxing, and extremely burdensome.

In contrast, the yoke of Jesus is easy. His way to God is not oppressive; his yoke is liberating. The yoke that binds you to God, in Christ, is not heavy.

God chases after you, not to strip away your freedoms, but to aggressively strip away the things that might oppress or enslave you. God is not seeking to burden or handicap you, but instead he is pursuing you so that you might have true freedom in him.

His yoke is easy! The Apostle John reiterates this: "His commandments are not burdensome" (1 John 5:3). If the version of the gospel you are preaching is burdensome, then it is not the gospel of Jesus Christ! Burdensome grace is not biblical grace.

Scent of Scandal

In his book *What's So Amazing about Grace?*, Philip Yancey recounts a story about an Australian convict who murdered a fellow inmate while serving a life sentence at a maximum security prison. Apparently, the convict had lost hope for living and simply wanted to die. He killed an inmate with the knowledge that he himself would then be executed. When asked why he had murdered the other inmate instead of just committing suicide, the man answered, "Well, I figure it's like this . . . I'm a Catholic. If I commit suicide I'll go straight to hell. But if I murder I can come back here to Sydney and confess to a priest before my execution. That way, God will forgive me."[1]

This Australian prisoner isn't the only person seeking to exploit the apparent "loophole" in grace. Is there potential for "grace abuse" when people hear this message? Absolutely! Human beings will always look for ways to excuse or rationalize their own sin and folly. But that doesn't negate the power of grace, nor does it make grace any less real.

The imputation of righteousness is not negated simply because some human beings will seek to manipulate it. Quite the opposite. The fact that some will seek to manipulate the grace of God demonstrates how wicked we truly are, and our desperate need for imputed righteousness.

Some people question my understanding of grace, or at minimum they are thinking that there must be more to this story of grace.

> Burdensome grace is not biblical grace.

> The grace
> of God
> may appear
> scandalous.

But there isn't. There is no catch here. Once we believe, we are rescued and redefined, no strings attached. *Grace is NOT too good to be true!*

Yancey writes, "I have portrayed God as a lovesick father eager to forgive, and grace as a force potent enough to break the chains that bind us, and merciful enough to overcome differences between us. Depicting grace in such sweeping terms makes people nervous, and I concede that I have skated to the very edge of danger. I have done so because I believe the New Testament does too. . . . Grace has about it the scent of scandal."[2]

The grace of God may appear scandalous. It seems too simple that God will forgive us and love us, no matter what. But that is the truth! That is biblical grace.

The thing inside of you that drives you to want to earn the grace of God is the very thing that will keep you from enjoying grace.

A pastor friend of mine told me that he gets more negative e-mails after preaching about grace than any other topic. In fact, the more grace-filled the sermon is, the more vicious the e-mails tend to be. It seems that people freak out whenever preachers tell them that there is absolutely nothing they can do to earn what God is giving. Quite honestly, grace seems to bother many people. Many are uncomfortable with grace. Why? Author Steve Brown gives a great answer to this question:

> Christians do not trust freedom. They prefer the
> security of rules and self-imposed boundaries,
> which they tend to inflict on other Christians. Real

freedom means the freedom to be wrong as well
as right. Christianity often calls us to live beyond
the boundaries, bolstered by the assurance that we
cannot fall beyond God's love. Freedom is dangerous,
but the alternative is worse—boxing ourselves up
where we cannot celebrate our unique gifts and
express our joy in Christ.[3]

Our churches are filled with people who cannot truly get their minds around the concept that God's love is absolutely unconditional. Many more feel the pressure and burden of being a "good Christian" in order to please God. But you should not ever feel any such burden or pressure to perform. You do not need to do anything. God's approval and affection are gifts that he freely gives. It is all by his grace.

People tend to struggle with the idea of imputed righteousness. Many feel the need to justify themselves. We do things to earn value and right standing. Even people who don't believe in God are driven to quantify their own existence. People behave in accordance with their drive to earn status or approval from God or others, but it is often a subconscious act.

Ask yourself, honestly, why do you serve God? Consider the things you do for God or for your church or even for your family. Are your actions truly motivated by gratitude for grace? Or is there any part of you that maybe is trying to earn approval?

You cannot earn the approval of God. It is a gift, given to all believers—an act of grace. Embracing God's grace can be a very difficult task. We simply cannot shake the feeling that we must do something for God in exchange for his affection.

The bottom line: you can't earn it! God freely gave you his love and grace. God chose to rescue you. He has given us his righteousness. Nothing can negate that. Even when you fail and sin and make stupid decisions, his love and approval still remain.

Sometimes genuine believers are going to fail, even though we have walked with Jesus. Just look at Peter, Jesus' key protégé. Peter had walked with Jesus for more than three years, but he ended up denying him. He blew it big time. But Jesus' response is gracious. Jesus doesn't condemn Peter. He doesn't hold it over Peter's head. Jesus doesn't threaten to take away Peter's access to God. Jesus responds by lovingly inviting Peter to be a minister of the gospel. Jesus graciously invites Peter to be restored back to his purpose of being a disciple of Jesus and shepherding his sheep (John 21:15–25).

No matter what you do, the grace of God remains when you accept it. God's grace is readily available to you. He is always compassionate toward his people, standing ready to accept you, to wipe the slate clean and to throw your sins into the "depths of the sea" (Mic. 7:19).

Antinomianism: Not Preached Here

The grace of God is powerful enough to cover all of your sins, and God pours it out in abundance. In fact, the more you sin, the more God pours out his grace. Grace abounds wherever sin abounds (Rom. 5:20). The more sin you have in your life, the more grace it takes to cover all of your sins; therefore, God keeps pouring out more grace to ensure that all of your sins are indeed covered.

Preachers of biblical grace often are accused of *antinomi-anism*. Antinomianism is the concept that God doesn't care about sin and pours out his grace on our lives without any expectation that we change our behaviors. Antinomians claim that God's moral law is of no use, and they feel free to reject all socially established morality.

Antinomianism is not my message! I firmly believe that God hates sin and demands that it be punished! That's the reason for the cross! He hates sin and wants us to live righteously. However, my message certainly may be confused with anti-nomianism. Genuine biblical grace often closely appears to be antinomianism. The great twentieth-century Welsh preacher Martyn Lloyd-Jones noted:

> There is thus clearly a sense in which the message of "justification by faith only" can be dangerous, and likewise with the message that salvation is entirely of grace. . . .
>
> I would say to all preachers: If your preaching of salvation has not been misunderstood in that way, then you had better examine your sermons again, and you had better make sure that you really are preaching the salvation that is offered in the New Testament to the ungodly, to the sinner, to those who are enemies of God. There is this kind of dangerous element about the true presentation of the doctrine of salvation.[4]

Many times I have corresponded with people who are either offended or confused when they begin to understand imputed righteousness and justification. Many sincere people simply cannot believe that the gospel is that easy.

The idea of grace, available in abundance whenever we need it, just doesn't sit well with some people. It may even make them angry. That's because it is contrary to what feels natural. Grace is opposite of what sinful humanity wants. We want to achieve and earn our status. We want a way to earn our justification. But God knows we simply cannot do that. And that's what makes grace amazing—he doesn't give us what we want, he gives us what we need!

His love for you is not based upon your performance, but on the mere fact that you are his creation, and God's approval of you is based on the righteousness imputed to you. Refusing to embrace these truths will push you toward legalism and will devastate both your spiritual and emotional health.

We have made the gospel hard and laborious. Author, seminary professor, and international radio host Steve Brown wrote these powerful words: "Our problem is that we have taken the best news ever given to the world, run it through a 'religious' grid, and made something unpalatable out of it."[5]

Only by embracing imputed righteousness and justification can you ever truly be spiritually strong enough to overcome any and all sin patterns in your life. Knowing that you are righteous no matter how you behave will give you strength when you face trials or temptations. And that knowledge will inspire you to continually mature in your faith. Brown put it this way,

> The only people who get better are people that know
> that, if they never get better, GOD WILL LOVE

THEM ANYWAY. . . . God will not only love you if you don't get better, He'll teach you that getting better isn't the issue; His love is the issue.[6]

If you are a genuine believer, then you are always loved by God and you will always be in right standing with Him, even when you make stupid sinful choices. Even if you make Christians look bad, even when you're a hypocrite, even when you sin a lot, even when you sin big, and even when fail miserably . . . God still loves you unconditionally!!!

Only by understanding God's grace can you mature in your faith. Embracing grace will catapult you to overcoming the besetting sins, the guilt, and the shame that have held you back from the abundant life that God desires for you. Embracing grace is the first step to overcoming sin. It leads you to deeper intimacy with God and more satisfaction in him. And that satisfaction melts away the desire and natural tendency to keep sin in your life.

> Only by embracing imputed righteousness and justification can you ever truly be spiritually strong enough to overcome any and all sin patterns in your life.

Grace Abuse

But let's take this the step deeper. Some people, and perhaps even you for just one moment, will ask, "If God will forgive me no matter what, then what motivation do I have to stop sinning?" The book of Romans depicts for us the thrilling concepts of grace, righteousness, and justification. God's mercy toward his creation is simply mind-blowing. But as Yancey notes, these doctrines present a problem: "Why be good if you know in advance you will be forgiven? Why strive to be Just As God Wants when he accepts me Just As I Am?"[7]

The Apostle Paul addressed this head-on. In Romans 5, Paul writes that God's grace will abound, even when our sin abounds. But he immediately follows those statements with a bold and aggressive question: "What shall we say then? Are we to continue in sin that grace may abound?" (Rom. 6:1). He answers with a fiery: "By no means!" The King James Version says: "God forbid!"

God forbid that any one of us go on sinning just because we know grace will be there when we need it. Yes, God will always forgive, but the knowledge of grace should not ever be an excuse to sin. Quite the opposite, the tremendous grace of God ought to motivate us and inspire us to love God more and to live righteously for him!

Later in Romans 6, Paul again asks the same question, and yet again gives the same fiery answer: "What then? Are we to sin because we are not under law but under grace? By no means!" (v. 15).

Grace ought to be the thing that makes us want to obey the teachings and commands of Jesus. Any person who feels encouraged to sin by grace has grossly misunderstood the nature and power of grace. This is why the Apostle Paul gave such an explosive response to the idea of grace abuse. Paul simply could not fathom someone becoming a follower of Christ and then choosing to simply continue a lifestyle of sin without regard to holy living. In his mind, that was just not an option:

How can we who died to sin still live in it? Do you not know that all of us who have been baptized into Christ Jesus were baptized into his death? We were buried therefore with him by baptism into death, in order that, just as Christ was raised from the dead by the glory of the Father, we too might walk in newness of life.

For if we have been united with him in a death like his, we shall certainly be united with him in a resurrection like his. We know that our old self was crucified with him in order that the body of sin might be brought to nothing, so that we would no longer be enslaved to sin. For one who has died has been set free from sin. (vv. 2–7)

In Paul's mind, there was simply no way for someone to "die to sin" without walking into "the newness of life" and out of the sinful life that binds us.

Do Whatever You Please

As I ponder the words of the Apostle Paul in Romans 6, I am reminded of recent conversation I had with a friend. He was telling me about a sermon that he had heard several years earlier. Apparently, he did not approve of the premise of that particular sermon. My friend seemed quite surprised with both the title and content of the sermon. The sermon had been entitled, "Love God, and live however the hell you want!" Certainly, that was an interesting start to any sermon. But more interesting was the fact that I absolutely and boldly agreed with that premise.

I believe that there are two things that Jesus wants Christians to do. First, love God with all your heart! Second, do whatever you want!

Now, when I make these types of comments, many people are both shocked and offended. They tell me, "No, God tells us to change and live righteously. We can't just do whatever we want and be sinful." My response is always the same, "When I tell you to live however you want to live, why do you assume that I am referring to a sinful lifestyle?"

If you truly follow the first thing I propose (that is, of course, to love God), then you will want to live for God. If you truly love God, your heart will change and desire the things of God. Therefore, when you chose to live however you want, you will want to seek God in all you do and you will live righteously in turn. If you truly love God, the "want" inside of you will want to please him and show the love of God to others. The fourth-century apologist and theologian St. Augustine of Hippo once wrote these powerful and controversial words: "Love God and do whatever you please. For the soul trained in love to God will do nothing to offend the One who is Beloved."[8] People who truly love God will seek to avoid the things that offend or dishonor God! I think that is what Paul was referring to. If you truly love God, how can you possibly go on living in sin? If you are a follower of Jesus, how can you possibly go a long period of time deliberately choosing to disobey the God you claim to serve?

I am not afraid to tell people to live however they want. In fact, I greatly encourage *all* people to live however they want to live. Living this way will truly expose whatever is ruling your heart and private thoughts. Living "however the hell you want" will expose your inward desires, showing the world whether or not your faith truly governs your heart. Doing "as you please" will demonstrate how much you truly love God, if you truly love him at all!

Ask yourself these questions: "If I truly lived as I pleased, what would my behavior look like? If I actually lived however I wanted, would God be honored in my actions?" If "whatever you please" dishonors God, then there is a significant problem with the quality and quantity of your love for God.

True Freedom in Christ

One of the biggest tragedies in the church today is that we often call people to fix their behaviors and alter their lifestyles without first teaching them to love God or helping them understand why they ought to love God.

Many preachers do not preach the freedom in Christ that we have. They fear that people will abuse it. However, the lack of preaching about freedom in Christ is precisely what leads people to feel *obligated* to believe in God, rather than *wanting* to believe in God. We should not feel obliged to obey the Bible; we should desire to obey the Bible!

How can I not preach the freedom that Jesus Christ has given us? How can I ignore one of the greatest gifts purchased for us by Christ? We cannot abstain from preaching the truth from God's Word because we are afraid of how some people might twist it or abuse it! Can you

> We often call people to fix their behaviors and alter their lifestyles without first teaching them to love God.

105

imagine if Jesus had taken that approach? What if Jesus had feared teaching truth because some of the people in the crowd might not respond properly? Where would we be right now?

We cannot avoid embracing truth simply because we are afraid of it! Instead, let us boldly and accurately preach the truth and let's trust God to use the truth to supernaturally minister to the people listening.

If someone takes the grace of God as a license to sin, that is the evidence that they do not love God, are probably not true believers, and are in need of understanding why God is worthy of being loved.

It is only by the grace of God and the enlightenment of the Holy Spirit that any of us realizes God's love for us. It is by the same grace and supernatural enlightenment that we realize our need for God. The realization that I needed God combined with the understanding that he had already taken the steps to fill that need in my life caused me to fall *in* love with him. The realization that God had been pursuing me all the days of my life caused me to want to know him intimately. And the realization of his awesomeness and his majesty caused me to revere him and fear him. God's love captured my heart. He swept me off my feet. And because of those realizations, I believe in him.

It is my love of God that causes me to follow him daily. So, with that in mind, do you honestly think that a preacher telling me that I have the freedom to sin would ever inspire me to go out and sin?!

If a preacher told me that I was obligated to obey the Bible, that wouldn't cause me to sin any less. Someone telling me I had better live righteously does nothing to help me to actually live right. In the same manner, someone telling me that I have the freedom to disobey does not cause me to want to sin. When you truly love God, his freedom doesn't inspire you to sin at all. It allows you to know that when you do sin or fail, you don't have to feel guilty or ashamed. You were free to sin. And after your sin, you are free to ask for forgiveness without any strings attached or any special penance.

Any desire I have within me to do what is right originates from the Holy Spirit that is now at work within me. My desire to do right never came from any sermon that proclaimed I was obligated to obey the Bible. The opposite is true, too. Likewise, my desire to sin never came from anyone telling me Christ set me free from all rules. I was born with the desire to sin. Nothing that any preacher could ever say would cause me to want to sin more or less. Some people may twist their understanding of grace as a justification and rationalization for their own desire to sin, but grace does not cause the desire to sin. The desire to sin has been there all along. But for those of us who do indeed genuinely love God, we will find great joy in knowing his freedom, and that will inspire us to obey his commands.

Just think about it. Which is more inspiring: A god who says you must obey, or a god who says you are completely free? And which person are you more likely to respond to: The person who tells you that you must do it, or the person who calls you to do it out of a spirit of gratitude and love?

Another pastor friend of mine recently posted this comment on his Facebook page: "I'm told that if I preach too much on God's love, people will be careless about sin. But twenty-five years of pastoring tells me that is NOT true." I wholeheartedly agree! Telling people about the unconditional love of God will not cause them to want to run toward sin, it will cause them to want to know more about the Creator who lovingly invites us to be restored.

I recognize God's immense love for me, and that causes me to love him. I want to serve God, but that desire in me is driven by my love for God, not any sense of obligation. Everything he has ever done for me is motivated by love. I desire to live a holy life that will make God look good. The motivation for any service or obedience I offer to God is simply an act of gratitude for the wondrous exchange. I am thankful for the cross and I love God!

Well, if I claim to have the freedom to choose obedience to Christ, then a plausible question arises: "Do I have freedom to disobey Christ if I so choose?" The natural thought pattern, when examining freedom, is to wonder what freedom's options are. God has given us his power to overcome sin, but are we obligated to defeat sin? I now have the freedom to choose to avoid sin, but do I have the freedom to choose to engage in sin? The question arises, "If I can't freely choose to do wrong, is that really freedom at all?" Brown explained it in this way:

> Not only do we know the truth about what God
> wants us to do, He provides the power to do it. If we
> don't have the freedom not to do what He wants,
> however, we have redefined the word "freedom."[9]

Jesus Christ set us free—he gave us true freedom. So YES, that means the freedom to choose to sin. We have the freedom to sin and it does not risk our standing as righteous in God's sight.

Christ set us free so that we might be free (Gal. 5:1). Christ wants us to be free—free to choose how we'd live our own lives. He purchased this freedom for us at the cross. We can choose to use the freedom however we like. We can do whatever we please.

Many people oppose the idea that Christ set us free to do whatever we want. Many Christians simply do not trust freedom. They see it as dangerous. Oftentimes, Christians prefer rules and limits. It makes them feel safe and secure. Many believers cling to their own self-imposed boundaries more tightly than they cling to Jesus.

> Many Christians simply do not trust freedom. They see it as dangerous.

Freedom is certainly dangerous, but the alternative is far worse: *legalism*. Legalism is anything that over-emphasizes the things we must do for Christ, focusing on behavior and conduct. Legalism concentrates on obeying rules and fulfilling expectations, instead of simply concentrating on the right thing: intimacy with the Savior, who calls us to live beyond the boundaries of legalism.

The freedom we have in Christ is real freedom—meaning we have the freedom to be wrong as well as right. Yes, God has given us the freedom to choose between obedience and disobedience ... and we can make either choice we want, without ever risking our status as justified before God. As Steve Brown wrote:

> *You are really and truly and completely free.*
> There is no kicker. There is no if, and, or but. You are free. You can do it right or wrong. You can obey or disobey. . . . You can choose to become a faithful

> Christian or an unfaithful Christian. You can cry,
> cuss, and spit, or laugh, sing, and dance. You can read
> a novel or the Bible. You can watch television or pray.
> You're free . . . really free.[10]

You have been set free in Christ. No limits, no boundaries. We are not saved by our own performance, but only by grace. *If my lack of sin could not earn my justification, how could my abundance of sin erase my status as justified?* I have absolute freedom in Christ; my behavior has no bearing on my status in God's kingdom as righteous or on my status in his family as his child.

I am fully aware that some people will read my words and misunderstand me, assuming that I am devaluing the ugliness or gravity of sin. I am *not* excusing sin. Sin is devastating to our lives and disgusting to God. He hates it. I am not preaching about imputed righteousness because I believe sin is okay. I preach about imputed righteousness because it is the truth, and because only by embracing truth will we ever be strong enough to overcome sin. Understanding grace helps us to be more successful as we wage war against sin. Sometimes, after preaching about the imputation of righteousness and justification, I have been asked, "Then why should I live for God?" or "If I am secure in my position with God, why don't I just go out and sin? Why even try?" The answer to these questions is quite simple: *because you love God!*

We follow his commands because we love him, not because we're obligated. We obey him because we trust him, not because we are forced to. We have absolute, total freedom in Christ to choose to live however we want to live our lives.

We are not required to obey his commands; we have the opportunity to obey his commands. If you love God, you will want to follow him and you will want to live for him! If you don't desire to live for God, then you don't genuinely love God. If you don't love God, then you're not truly born again! *Any person willing to use his freedom in Christ for sin probably is not a sincere believer in Christ . . . hmmmm????*

What Is True Repentance?

After preaching these concepts, I have often been asked, "But, what about repentance?" Let me make it clear: *I believe in repentance!* The seventeenth-century English poet Francis Quarles wrote, "He that hath promised pardon on our repentance hat not promised life till we repent."[11] God has certainly promised to forgive us upon our repentance, but we must first, of course, actually repent. Many times throughout both the Old and New Testaments, people are called to repent. John the Baptist was famous for proclaiming, "Repent, for the kingdom of heaven is at hand" (Matt. 3:2).

But what is true repentance? Oftentimes, preachers may refer to repentance as turning away from sin or changing our behaviors. We often associate repentance with altering our lifestyles. This is a misunderstanding of *repentance*. The original word in the New Testament that we often translate as repent is the Greek word *metanoeō*. When literally translated, this word means, "changing of the mind."[12] Repentance is not changing your actions; repentance is changing your mind. And naturally, of course, after someone has genuinely changed their mind, their actions will soon follow.

> Repentance is not changing your actions; repentance is changing your mind.

Allow me to use one of my favorite foods to illustrate. I used to frequent Applebees at least twice a week. I loved their boneless buffalo wings. My opinion was that Applebees had the absolute best boneless buffalo wings in the United States, and I am a *huge* fan of boneless buffalo wings. But then, one day, I discovered a new restaurant called Buffalo Wild Wings (more affectionately known as "B-dubs"). After trying the boneless wings at B-dubs, my mind changed. Now I believe B-dubs is the best. And that mind change has led to a shift in my actions as well. Now when I crave wings, I don't go to Applebees; I go to B-dubs.

The changing of my mind made me a "believer." That was the repentance; a genuine shift or change in my thinking, my opinion, and my sincerely held belief. Then, the repentance yielded some change in my actions. I did not need to force myself to change my behavior. When your mind is changed, your behaviors will naturally change too.

Okay, maybe my affection for buffalo wings is a bit of a stretch as a good analogy to illustrate biblical repentance. Let's examine a situation, with much bigger ramifications, about a friend of mine named Nelson.

Nelson was dating a gal named Kimberly. Nelson was crazy about her. He often couldn't stop talking about how great she was. But one day Kimberly broke it off. It came as a surprise to me, but surely it was her prerogative to move on from the relationship.

The thing that was very odd was the fact that, even after the breakup, the two of them still spent a lot of time together. Long phone calls, going to restaurants together, and even physical intimacy. This went on for a few months.

Eventually, Nelson met Abigail. When Abigail was new on the scene, Nelson would go on and on about her. He often compared her to Kimberly, making his opinion clear that Abigail was a far better person. Nelson claimed that he was no longer in love with Kimberly and now he was totally in love in Abigail. He was professing a change of heart and mind.

Nelson had been a believer that Kimberly was the best girl for him, but now his opinion changed. He had previously been convinced that Kimberly was the greatest girl, but now Abigail had caused him to believe differently. This is a form of repentance.

How do we know if the change of his mind was genuine? If Nelson's repentance was legitimate, we should expect to see a shift in his actions, too. Genuine repentance always yields change in actions. If Nelson had really fallen in love with Abigail, then we would not need to force him to change his behavior. It would happen naturally.

Well, I'm sure you've guessed it . . . Nelson's actions would eventually show that his opinion had not really changed. Nelson proclaimed that Abigail was the best, but he continued to keep a relationship with Kimberly that showed something very different. Against my advice, he continued to have an emotional affair with her. He continued to spend time with her and eventually it led to a physical affair, as well. His heart and mind were clearly still set on Kimberly. Do I believe that Nelson's mind was ever really changed? Not at all! Not based on what I observed.

If Nelson told you that he loved Abigail with all his heart, would you believe him? Of course not! You would probably call him a liar. Nelson said one thing with his mouth, but did another with his actions. You might even be inclined to call him a hypocrite!

Obviously, Nelson did indeed have some level of interest in Abigail, but he clearly had not ever truly had any real heart or mind change about Kimberly. If he really had any change in his mind and heart, then his actions would have been different. I think Nelson gives us a glimpse into how many people approach God.

There are plenty of people who live their lives on their own terms until one day they come to some knowledge of God and make a profession of faith in Christ. They have some legitimate interest in God and their profession of faith may even seem to be legitimate for a while. But their hearts are still set on the things of this world. Their beliefs do not lead to radical obedience to the commands of Scripture. Their minds have not fully shifted. They have not truly trusted in Christ and do not love him wholeheartedly. Eventually, actions demonstrate the reality of beliefs. Our behaviors do not determine our righteousness, but they sure do authenticate (or in many cases expose) the level of our beliefs.

Someone who claims to be a follower of Jesus but does not follow the teachings of Jesus is a liar and a hypocrite. The Apostle John said it best:

And by this we know that we have come to know him, if we keep his commandments. Whoever says "I know him" but does not keep his commandments is a liar, and the truth is not in him, but whoever keeps his word, in him truly the love of God is perfected. By this we may know that we are in him. (1 John 2:3–5)

If someone claims to love God but there is not any genuine lifestyle modification, then that is a clear indication the person does not truly love God and probably has not ever truly been born again. Someone who has claimed to be a believer but does not show it with his actions probably has not ever truly been born again. The profession of faith was not genuine.

Repentance is a changing of the mind. When you repent before God, you are changing your mind about what you think about God. You believe in him—not only in his existence, but also in his trustworthiness. You are now acknowledging that God is right and that his words are true.

After repentance, we believe that God's ways are best; therefore, we choose to follow them. After repentance, we believe serving God is best; therefore, we serve him. Genuine belief in God leads us to change our lifestyles, our behaviors, and our choices to be in line with what we believe about God.

God gives us total freedom to choose to live however we want to live our lives. The true believer knows he can live however he wants to live and can do whatever he pleases. Being that the true believer loves God, he will choose to live righteously, as Jesus commanded. The genuine believer wants to do the right thing. Fake believers don't want to do the right thing;

they believe they are obligated to do the right thing. There is a gigantic difference!

The believer may have moments and even seasons of life where sin and failure are prevalent, but the true believer will always come back to God and will attempt to live better, as God empowers him to do so. However, the beauty of God's grace is that even if the believer doesn't live better, he will still be loved and accepted by God.

A Response to Freedom in Christ

God is inviting us to use our freedom to live righteously, to honor Christ. I love God so I plan to respond to that invitation. You may do whatever you please with your freedom, but my recommendation: *live for God!*

In the Old Testament, Joshua made a similar challenge to the Jewish people:

> Choose this day whom you will serve, whether the gods your fathers served in the region beyond the River, or the gods of the Amorites in whose land you dwell. But as for me and my house, we will serve the LORD. (Josh. 24:15)

We are free, truly free. But what an insane thought it is to use our freedom to continually sin. Sin has had devastating effects on my life. Why would I ever want to intentionally subject myself to that again! That would be true insanity! We are free to choose whatever we want, but those people who love God understand how awesome it is to live for him. With this in mind, I encourage all of us to make every effort to perform well for him, but always remember that we do not do it because we are obligated, but because we want to be more like the one we love so much—Jesus Christ.

God has freed us from having to suffer the eternal consequences of sin, so why would we ever want to continue to live in sin and be forced to suffer the devastating consequences that sin could have in this life? We live for God because we love him and we are so thankful for the grace he has bestowed upon us.

We are free to choose obedience. We are free to live in accordance with the righteousness imputed to us. And we are empowered by God to actually live for Him. It is God who will indeed give us the power to live the right way. God will sustain us as we seek to live righteously:

> He will keep you steadfast in the faith to the end, so that when his day comes you need fear no condemnation. God is utterly dependable, and it is he who has called you into fellowship with his Son Jesus Christ, our Lord. (1 Cor. 1:8–9 PHILLIPS)

God gives us the power to overcome sin. God's power is at work within us to help us be more like Christ.

God desires that we stop sinning. We press on daily, seeking to live right and defeat sin, through God's grace and power. But even when we do sin and fail, we can be confident our status has not changed. Consider these words from the Apostle John:

> My little children, I am writing these things to you so that you may not sin.

> God's power is at work within us to help us be more like Christ.

117

Redefined

> But if anyone does sin, we have an advocate with
> the Father, Jesus Christ the righteous. He is the
> propitiation for our sins, and not for ours only but
> also for the sins of the whole world. (1 John 2:1–2)

Here John makes it clear: avoiding sin should be a priority in our lives. "But if anybody does sin," we do not have to worry or ever feel ashamed because we know that we have someone who will speak on our behalf—Jesus Christ! Again, the goal of our lives ought to be to get rid of all sin, but if and when the time comes that you miss the goal, you can remain confident. Your record remains perfect in his eyes!

It is completely your choice to follow his moral laws. Being obedient to God's moral laws is fully your choice, not an obligation; therefore, there is no need to feel guilty when you fail. When we blow it, we simply ask God for forgiveness, and we keep going, with absolute confidence in his tremendous love!

So, I ask the question: Is grace a license to sin? *Of course not!* That's just silly. Grace most certainly has a scent of scandal about it, but that's what makes it so amazing and so confounding! There is nothing more amazing than the glorious grace of God!

Endnotes

1. Phillip Yancy, *What's So Amazing about Grace?* (Grand Rapids: Zondervan, 2002), 177.

2. Ibid., 178.

3. Steve Brown, *A Scandalous Freedom: The Radical Nature of the Gospel* (West Monroe: Howard, 2004), 102.

4. Martyn Lloyd-Jones, *Romans: Exposition of Chapter 6* (Carlisle, PA: The Banner of Truth Trust, 1989), 9.

5. Brown, *A Scandalous Freedom*, 68.

6. Ibid., 46 (emphasis mine).

7. Yancey, *What's So Amazing*, 185.

8. Matt Slick, *"Augustine of Hippo (354-430)"* CARM, accessed January 1, 2014, http://carm.org/augustine#footnote8_tmjod82.

9. Brown, *A Scandalous Freedom*, 9.

10. Ibid., 12.

11. Elon Foster, *New Cyclopædia of Prose Illustrations: Adapted to Christian Teaching; Embracing Mythology, Analogies, Legends, Parables, Emblems, Metaphors, Similes, Allegories, Proverbs; Classic, Historic, and Religious Anecdotes, Etc., Volume 1* (New York: Funk & Wagnall, 1872), 554.

12. Sowing Circle, Inc., *Blue Letter Bible*, "Greek Lexicon::G3341 (KJV)." accessed February 9, 2013, http://www.blueletterbible.org/lang/lexicon/lexicon.cfm?Strongs=G3341&t=KJV.

Chapter 6

Abba's Child

Human beings are enamored with the idea of having a great dad. That's why the most popular television shows have been focused on the interactions of dads with their families. Who didn't love Dr. Heathcliff Huxtable and John Walton and Mike Brady and Ward Cleaver? Who would turn down having Jim Anderson or Charles Ingalls as their daddy? And who didn't adore neat-freak Danny Tanner and the wise ole' Reverend Eric Camden?

We love dads; it's in our DNA. Well, when we are born again, we are declared to be God's children! You now have the greatest daddy ever!

The moment you were born again, you were redefined. You are now his kid. And God desires to have a magnificent love relationship with each one of his children. You were created to experience his daddy nature. He longs to be a great daddy to you, to spend time with you, to comfort you, to teach you things, to be your source of rest.

Imagine this: a man comes home from a long day of work and plops down on the couch. His adorable four-year-old daughter runs up to him, yelling with insurmountable joy, "Daddy, Daddy, Daddy! You're home!" She then, without regard to his exhaustion, boldly climbs up onto the sofa and jumps right into his lap. She puts her head on his chest to listen to her daddy's heartbeat. Her head slowly bobs upward and downward with each breath he takes.

He's had a long day at work and he needs some alone time, but he doesn't resent this moment one bit. In fact, this renews and rejuvenates him. He wraps his arms around her and says, "Oh sweetheart, I missed you today. How was your day?" She tells him of all her adventures that day. She tells him about the doll she dressed, the grilled cheese sandwich she ate for lunch, and all the odd people she saw at the mall. After a brief moment of silence, she quietly says, "Daddy, I love you!"

This is the love relationship God desires to have with you. You can jump up into his lap anytime. *God, the greatest daddy ever, wishes to wrap his loving arms around you. He wants to embrace you!* We are children in God's family. Our adoption into God's family opens the doors to the warmth of God's loving embrace.

God's Royal Family

Thus far we have thoroughly examined the imputation of righteousness and explored our amazing freedom in Christ. There is another amazing legal position given to us through simple belief in the person of Christ. We are declared to be members of God's royal family. We are now a part of an eternal legacy. We have an inheritance! The Apostle Paul makes it clear that we are heirs to the King! *We are the royalty.*

> For all who are led by the Spirit of God are sons of God. For you did not receive the spirit of slavery to fall back into fear, but *you have received the Spirit of adoption* as sons, by whom we cry, "Abba! Father!" The Spirit himself bears witness with our spirit that *we are children of God, and if children, then heirs— heirs of God and fellow heirs with Christ,* provided we suffer with him in order that we may also be glorified with him. (Rom. 8:14–17, emphasis mine)

Take this for example: I was born into the Ortiz family. On the day of my birth, I became a member of that family. The name "Ortiz" was pronounced upon me by my father. *I instantly became an heir to everything he owns.* I am entitled to inherit his estate—that is my legal right. I instantly became a co-heir with my older brother. I am entitled to share in the inheritance alongside him.

I know this is a simple illustration, but it represents a concept many believers seem to misunderstand. On the day of my spiritual birth, I was adopted into God's family. Scripture declares that I am a co-heir with Jesus Christ; he and I are brothers. God the Father labels me as his own son:

> For *in Christ Jesus you are all sons of God, through faith.* (Gal. 3:26, emphasis mine)

> God sent forth his Son, born of woman, born under the law, to redeem those who were under the law, so that we might *receive adoption* as sons. And because you are sons, God has sent the Spirit of his Son into our hearts, crying, "Abba! Father!" *So you are no longer a slave, but a son, and if a son, then an heir through God.* (Gal. 4:4–7, emphasis mine)

We are heirs of God the Father, and co-heirs with Christ. Through the cross, Jesus has earned the right to share his entitlement as heir with whomever he chooses and—praise God—Jesus has chosen to share that entitlement with us! Jesus Christ chose to elevate us from lowly sinners to righteous children of God. This status as children of God entitles us to all the things that God has promised us. Notice that I didn't say that this status entitles us to whatever we want, but rather this entitles us to whatever he wants to give us.

Now, some people get a little nervous when I say that we are *entitled* to certain things. But this should not make you nervous. If God has sovereignly declared that I am his heir, then who am I to argue with him? If God has sovereignly declared that I am a co-heir with Christ, who am I to tell him that I don't deserve that? If you are a genuine believer in Jesus, then you are definitely entitled to receive all the benefits of Sonship! You have been adopted by the Divine. The Creator of the universe calls you his child. Not because of anything you have done to deserve it or to merit it, but because of the precious work of Christ at the cross. Jesus purchased your right to be a child of God.

We are a part of God's family. We have been adopted into royalty, and the children of royalty are *always* entitled to being treated as royalty. The son of the king gets to enjoy the fruit of his father's labor. The son of the king gets to delight in all that the king has earned. We get to enjoy all that our king has earned on our behalf.

Adoption into divine royalty is purely an act of love and sovereign grace by God. It is God who chose us, before the beginning of time, to be a part of his royal family. The Apostle Paul referred to this in his letter to the church at Ephesus:

> For he chose us in him *before the creation* of the world *to be holy and blameless in his sight. In love he predestined us to be adopted as his sons through Jesus Christ*, in accordance with his pleasure and will— to the praise of his glorious grace, which has been freely given us in the One he loves. In him we have redemption through his blood, the forgiveness of sins, in accordance with the riches of God's grace that he lavished on us. . . .
>
> *When you believed, you were marked in him with a seal, the promised Holy Spirit, who is a deposit guaranteeing our inheritance.* (Eph. 1:4–7, 13–14 NIV, emphasis mine)

God bestows all the benefits of Sonship to all those who place their faith in Jesus Christ. The greatest benefits of Sonship are the salvation of our souls from the consequences of our own sin and the promise to spend eternity with him.

The Apostle Paul wrote these words to the Thessalonians:

> For you are all children of light, children of the day. We are not of the night or of the darkness. . . . For God has not destined us for wrath, but to obtain salvation through our Lord Jesus Christ. (1 Thess. 5:5, 9)

The Apostle John most certainly affirmed the thoughts and teachings of the Apostle Paul regarding our eligibility to call God our Father. He wrote this in his Gospel:

> But to all who did receive him, **who** *believed in his name, he gave the right to become children of God,* who were born, not of blood nor of the will of the flesh nor of the will of man, but of God. (John 1:12–13, emphasis mine)

Mark Brumley, managing editor of *Catholic Faith Magazine*, also spoke of the Fatherhood of God and benefits bestowed upon believers:

> Jesus tells His followers to address God as Father (Mt 6:9–13). . . .
>
> Elsewhere in the New Testament, God is also depicted as Father to Christians. Through Jesus Christ we are more than mere creatures to God; by faith in Him we become the children of God (1 Jn 5:1), sharing in Jesus' own Divine Sonship (Rom. 8:29).[1]

It is essential that you understand God's intimate love for you, and maybe even more essential that you genuinely embrace God as your father. Fatherhood is a characteristic of our God— he is our daddy! The greatest daddy ever!

J. I. Packer, one of the most influential evangelical authors of the twentieth century, believes that this is the key barometer for a believer's intimate knowledge of God. In his book *Knowing God*, he wrote these profound comments:

> If you want to judge how well a person understands
> Christianity, find out how much he makes of the
> thought of being God's child, and having God as
> his Father. If this is not the thought that prompts
> and controls his worship and prayers and his whole
> outlook on life, it means that he does not understand
> Christianity very well at all. For everything that
> Christ taught, everything that makes the New
> Testament new, and better than the Old, everything
> that is distinctively Christian as opposed to merely
> Jewish, is summed up in the knowledge of the
> Fatherhood of God. "Father" is the Christian name
> for God. . . . Our understanding of Christianity
> cannot be better than our grasp of adoption.[2]

If you do not embrace this truth, you will never accomplish all that God has ordained for you. Your understanding of divine adoption is a glass ceiling in your life. The more you understand it, the more likely you are to fulfill your potential, and more importantly, the more glory you will bring to God in your life.

The Fatherhood of God

God is referred to as Father more than 275 times throughout
Scripture. The message is obvious and overwhelming. God
himself desires to establish an intimate Father-child relationship with you. *In fact, intimacy is what you were created for.*

Only by understanding the Fatherhood of God can we find
our identity and our sense of self-worth. *Only when we experience God's Fatherly embrace can we begin to understand the
fierce love of God.* It is only through intimacy with the Almighty
that we can mature in our faith. And, most importantly, it is
only through intimacy with him that we can truly bring him
the maximum amount of glory possible!

God declares himself as our Father and he chooses to treat
us as a father treats a son. Moses declared to the Israelites, "Is
not he your father, who created you, who made you and established you?" (Deut. 32:6). And carefully consider the words of
the prophet Isaiah, "But now, O LORD, you are our Father; we
are the clay, and you are our potter; we are all the work of your
hand" (Isa. 64:8). The psalmist declared, "As a father shows
compassion to his children, so the LORD shows compassion to
those who fear him." (Ps. 103:13). Examine the words of Jesus
when instructing us how to pray. He taught us to start with
these precious words: "Our Father" (Matt. 6:9).

The classic author A. W. Tozer wrote this about God's
fatherly love toward us:

> He remembers our frame and knows that we are dust.
> He may sometimes chasten us, it is true, but even this
> He does with a smile, the proud, tender smile of a

Father who is bursting with pleasure over
an imperfect but promising son who is
coming every day to look more and more
like the One whose child he is.[3]

Even when God is disciplining us, he does so
with tremendous compassion toward us. Tozer's
proposal here is that God is "bursting with pleasure" as he deals with us—even in our folly and
even in our sin. This is inspiring! God is the perfect Father, and he is committed to helping us
mature into being more like him.

> Even when
> God is
> disciplining
> us, he does
> so with
> tremendous
> compassion
> toward us.

In the middle of the seventeenth century, a large group
of church leaders and pastors from all around England met
together regularly for a period of five years, at a place known
as Westminster Abbey. Through this series of meetings, three
of the most influential documents in all of modern church history were produced. The most influential was the *Westminster
Confession of Faith* (1646). This confession contains more than
twelve thousand words, but few of them are as dear as these:

All those that are justified, God vouchsafeth, in and
for his only Son Jesus Christ, to make partakers of
the grace of adoption: by which they are taken into
the number, and *enjoy the liberties and privileges of
the children of God*; have his name put upon them;
receive the Spirit of adoption; *have access to the
throne of grace with boldness; are enabled to cry,
Abba, Father*; are pitied, protected, provided for,
and chastened by his as by a father; yet never cast off,

129

but sealed to the day of redemption, and inherit the promises, as heirs of everlasting salvation.[4]

The word "vouchsafeth" (an old English word), according to Merriam's Dictionary, means "to grant something to someone in a gracious manner."[5] The Confession is declaring that God the Father has given a gift to all those who have been justified through Jesus Christ. The Confession then expounds on that gift. Notice the specific vernacular. We now have the ability to be "partakers of the grace of adoption" and we have the right to "enjoy the liberties and privileges of the children of God." The Confession affirms our rights to refer to God as our daddy, the free access we have to approach the "throne of grace with boldness," the privilege bestowed upon us of having "his name put upon us," as well as our rights to be "pitied, protected, provided for, and chastened." These rights are granted to "all those that are justified."

On September 12, 1858, the great preacher and theologian Charles Spurgeon (my absolute favorite preacher from all of church history) preached one of his most influential sermons. It was entitled "The Fatherhood of God," and it was delivered at London's Surrey Gardens Music Hall before a crowd of more than ten thousand people. Here are a few excerpts from that famous sermon:

> Let us rather draw near to the throne of the heavenly grace with boldness, as children coming to a father. . . .
>
> Some say that the fatherhood of God is universal and that every man, from the fact of his being created, is necessarily God's son. They say therefore

that every man has a right to approach the throne
of God, and say, "Our Father in heaven." With that
I must disagree. I believe that in this prayer we are
to come before God, looking upon Him not as our
Father through creation, but as our Father through
adoption and the new birth. . . .

This relationship also involves *love*. If God is
my Father, He loves me, and oh, how He loves me!
When God is a husband, He is the best of husbands.
Widows, somehow or other, are always well cared
for. When God is a friend, He is the best of friends
and sticks closer than a brother. And when He is a
Father, He is the best of fathers. . . .

*The fatherhood of God is common to all His
children.* . . . David was the son of God, but not more
the son of God than you. Peter and Paul, the highly
favored apostles, were of the family of the Most High.
And so are you. You have children yourselves—one
is a son grown up and out in business, perhaps, and
you have another, a little things still in arms. Which
is more your child, the little one or the big one? "Both
alike," you say. "This little one is my child near my
heart, and the big one is my child, too."

And so the little Christian is as much a child of
God as the great one. . . .

One may have more grace than another, but God
does not love one more than another. One may be an
older child than another, but he is not more a child.
One may do mightier works and may bring more

glory to his Father, but he whose name is the least in the kingdom of heaven is as much the child of God as he who stands among the king's mighty men. Let this cheer and comfort us when we draw near to God and say, "Our Father in heaven."

I will make but one more remark before I leave this point, namely, this: that *our being the children of God brings with it innumerable privileges*. Time would fail me if I were to attempt to read the long roll of the Christian's joyous privileges. . . .

And what is the spirit of adoption by which we cry out, "Abba, Father" (Rom. 8:15)? I cannot tell you. But if you have felt it, you will know it. It is a sweet compound of faith that knows God to be my Father, love that loves Him as my Father, joy that rejoices in Him as my Father, fear that trembles to disobey Him because He is my Father, and a confident affection and trustfulness that relies upon Him and casts itself wholly upon Him, because it knows by the infallible witness of the Holy Spirit that Jehovah, the God of earth and heaven, is the Father of my heart.

Oh, have you ever felt the spirit of adoption? There is nothing like it beneath the sky![6]

> God's love for his children is extravagant and unfathomable.

Spurgeon's enthusiasm is contagious. I particularly loved the exclamation, "Oh, how he loves me!" The first time I read this I was overwhelmed with emotion. Oh, how God loves me! He loves me, like a good daddy loves his own child!

God loves us just as much as he loves the biblical greats like David and Paul and Peter and every other great person of faith that we look up to. We are a part of the same heritage that they were. Not because of anything we have done to earn this, but because God adopted us into his family! And he has done this for us because he loves us!

God's love for his children is extravagant and unfathomable. Author and theologian Sam Storms wrote this in a blog:

> Notwithstanding what you have been told in the past or what you may feel in the present, when God thinks about you, feels for you, and sees you, He opens His mouth and sings with inexpressible joy!
>
> God's love for you is so infinitely intense that He quite literally sings for joy. The depth of His affection is such that mere words prove paltry and inadequate. So profoundly intimate is God's devotion to you that He bursts forth in sacred song. I'm talking about you. That's right, *you*, not just all the other people reading this article. I'm talking about each and every one of you who is convinced that no matter how many times I tell you God loves *you*, still you imagine He must have someone else in mind.
>
> No, He has *you* in mind.[7]

We Cry, "Abba! Father!"

We have the right to cry out "Abba! Father!" Twice in his letters, the Apostle Paul makes reference to *"Abba! Father!"* (Rom. 8:15; Gal. 4:6). The word "Abba" comes from the Aramaic language. It is a term of great endearment used by a child to address his father, similar to "papa" or "daddy,"[8] but Abba goes beyond either of those. There is no adequate English equivalent for this term. It is the most personal and most intimate form of paternal address.

The fact that the Apostle Paul specifically uses the Aramaic word in these passages in lieu of a Greek equivalent is significant. The New Testament was written in Greek because it was the official diplomatic and trade language of the first century, but the common language of the region was Aramaic. Greek was formal while Aramaic was casual. It is no accident that Paul uses the more casual language here. I believe Paul wanted to give his readers a more comfortable and intimate emotion, as if he wanted to purposely make the point that we can feel comfortable with God, we can be intimate with God. We can use casual lingo. We can feel at ease with him, we can feel safe to be ourselves around him. There is only one reference in the New Testament to Jesus using the Aramaic term "Abba." It was the night before he died on the cross. He was praying in a garden, and it is here that we are given a unique window into a very vulnerable moment:

> He fell on the ground and prayed that, if it were possible, the hour might pass from him. And he said, "Abba, Father, all things are possible for you. Remove this cup from me. Yet not what I will, but what you will." (Mark 14:35–36)

Jesus asks the Father to somehow save him from the impending torture he is about to endure. Jesus seems to be looking for a way out of dying on the cross. Almost as if he didn't want to go through it. Jesus knew what was coming, and he was asking the Father for a way out of it. It is here that he says, "Abba!"

At his greatest time of need, in his greatest moment of angst, he cried out "Abba!" In the moment where he felt most alone, when he most needed comfort from the Father—Jesus cried out "Abba!" Let this be an example to us. *In our greatest time of need, when we most need comfort, cry out to him. Cry out "Daddy!"*

After his prayer to the Father, Jesus then submits to the will of his Father. He basically says, "Oh Daddy, I need you! Yes Father, if there was a way to save these people without dying on the cross, then I would ask you to do that instead of this, but if this is what you want me to do, then I will do it." In this passage, Jesus is modeling our ability to approach the Father as our daddy.

God is our daddy, and as such, we can be confident that he hears us, and he longs to spend time with us and be intimate with us. As a child of God, you don't have to beg God to hear and answer your prayers. You don't have to wonder if he wants to spend time with you. As Abba's child, you have the right to stand boldly in his presence and be confident that he hears you.

This is who you are—Abba's child. Many sincere believers suffer from a horrific case of mistaken identity. They define themselves as undeserving slaves rather than adopted children. The late Franciscan priest Brennan Manning wrote this simple but powerful challenge: "Define yourself radically as one beloved by God. This is the true self. Every other identity is illusion."[9]

How do you answer this simple question: "Who are you?" The appropriate answer is not your name or your occupation or your achievements. You are not first and foremost a parent or spouse. I am not a pastor or teacher or writer or whatever other labels that can be placed on me. I believe in Christ, therefore I am first and foremost a child of the King. Will you define yourself with the labels projected upon you by society, or will you choose to define yourself with the labels pronounced upon you by God in his Word? He is our Abba and we are his children! Will you believe it? Will you embrace it?

Our status as children of the King endows us with certain unalienable divine rights—mostly, the right to enjoy the Father's company and protection in our greatest times of angst, even in the midst of our greatest sin. Our failures, transgressions, and problems do not negate our status as children of the King. When a butterfly fails, it doesn't somehow get turned back into a caterpillar. In the same way, our status in the royal family is not determined by our abilities, but by Christ.

Remember the time when you were a kid and you fell and scraped your knee. What was the response? We would always bolt directly into mama's or daddy's arms, knowing they'd make it better, right? We didn't run away from them when we fell, did we? Of course not! So why is it that we run from God when we fall? Our confidence in God should never be shaken by our circumstances or even by our own failures and sins, no matter how big they might be. Nothing can separate us from the love of Christ:

Who shall separate us from the love of Christ? Shall tribulation, or distress, or persecution, or famine, or nakedness, or danger, or sword?

No, in all these things we are more than conquerors through him who loved us. For I am sure that neither death nor life, nor angels nor rulers, nor things present nor things to come, nor powers, nor height nor depth, nor anything else in all creation, will be able to separate us from the love of God in Christ Jesus our Lord. (Rom. 8:35, 37–39)

I am convinced that God hates how often we allow our own sins to stop us from approaching him. Manning put it this way: "God's sorrow lies in our refusal to approach Him when we have sinned and failed."[10]

Our sin should never hinder our confidence to run toward him. Your failures cannot and will not negate his Daddy love for you! Your Heavenly Daddy always longs for you to run to him when you are in need, even when your need is caused by your own disobedience or folly.

Whenever we run to God with a need or we come to him asking for forgiveness, he responds the same way a good parent responds to their child who is genuinely sorry. God is moved with compassion and chooses to wipe the slate clean. That is our Daddy!

The Daddy-Shaped Hole in Our Hearts

We are all greatly affected by our relationships with our parents—particularly our fathers. Today, I have developed a good relationship with my earthly father, but growing up, our relationship wasn't so great. When I first became a Christian in my teenage years, I found it hard to see God as my Daddy. I loved the idea of having God as my best friend, my guide, and my Lord, but the concept of God as a daddy was something I rejected.

Then, during my mid-twenties, I made the staggering discovering that *we are all created for a relationship with our Heavenly Daddy.* The more of his love we experience, the more we are inspired to worship him. More intimacy with the Almighty God causes us to be more likely to obey his commands. The more of God's love we encounter, the more we are emboldened in our service to others. Ultimately, more love from him leads to more glory for him in our lives. We need God!

We are all born with a daddy-shaped hole in our hearts, and it is God alone who has the ability to fill that hole. But early in life, our initial exposure to daddies happens to be our earthly fathers. This is where things can go awry.

We often project onto our Heavenly Father whatever it is we happen to believe about our earthly fathers. Whether you had a great or terrible father growing up, the very fact that your dad is human guarantees that, at some point in your life, he hurt you or frustrated you or disappointed you.

If your earthly father was distant toward you, then you probably subconsciously assume that God is distant. If your dad didn't show up to your baseball games, your dance recitals, or your school plays because he was too busy, then you most likely feel like God is too busy for you. If your dad was abusive, then it is very possible that a part of you is expecting God to eventually violate or abuse you. If your father abandoned you, then you probably have a sense that it's only a matter of time before God abandons you. Or maybe your biological dad died when you were young. It probably wasn't his own fault, but you've been subconsciously frustrated with him for not being there for you. If so, these are ill feelings you probably have unknowingly projected onto God.

> God is not a reflection of your earthy father; instead, God is the perfection of your earthly father.

Oftentimes, whatever we experienced with our biological fathers is what we will expect from God. But this is not true. *God is not a reflection of your earthy father; instead, God is the perfection of your earthly father.*

Imagine if all your dad's good qualities were magnified and all his bad qualities were instantly sliced away. What an awesome person you would have. With this image in mind, you're starting to glimpse God the Father!

Take some time to think about any and all ill feelings you may have toward your dad for something he did. It is essential to begin to truly realize and embrace the fact that God is not like your earthly father. God will never hurt you in the same way. God will never abandon you, God will never violate you, God is never too busy for you, God will always listen to you, God will never turn his back on you, and God will never betray you!

> For my father and my mother have forsaken me,
>   but the LORD will take me in. (Ps. 27:10)

> Father of the fatherless and protector of widows
>> is God in his holy habitation. (Ps. 68:5)

God wants to be your Daddy! He wants to be intimate with you. Your Heavenly Father desires for you to experience his wonderful loving embrace. He wants you to unashamedly jump up into his lap and allow him to embrace you. God wants you to confidently cry out "Abba!"

At the exact moment that you trusted in Christ, you underwent a marvelous metamorphosis and you were declared to be the righteousness of God. You were also labeled a child of the living God, an heir to the throne of the King of the universe. You have officially been adopted by God. You are a member of the royal family. You have done nothing to earn this gift of adoption—it was a gift, freely given to you by God himself!

When I meditate on these truths I am flooded with emotion and my eyes fill with tears. And I often cannot help but ask, "Why? . . . Why did God choose to do this for me?" The answer is quite simple. . . . He loves us!

> Let them thank the LORD for his steadfast love,
>> for his wondrous works to the children of man!
> For he satisfies the longing soul,
>> and the hungry soul he fills with good things.
> (Ps. 107:8–9)

> See what kind of love the Father has given to us, that
> we should be called children of God; and so we are.
> The reason why the world does not know us is that
> it did not know him. Beloved, we are God's children

now, and what we will be has not yet appeared; but
we know that when he appears we shall be like him,
because we shall see him as he is. (1 John 3:1–2)

You are a child of God. He is your Abba. And such, he promises
to deal with us in love. He guarantees us his acceptance and
approval.

Many believers have an image that God is waiting to
pounce on us for any little mistake we might make. Quite the
opposite is true. God always sees us as his beloved children. If
we fail, he is filled with compassion toward us.

> Yet he, being compassionate,
>   atoned for their iniquity
> and did not destroy them;
>   he restrained his anger often
> and did not stir up all his wrath.
>   He remembered that they were but flesh,
> a wind that passes and comes not again.
> (Ps. 78:38–39)

> For you, O Lord, are good and forgiving,
>   abounding in steadfast love to all who call upon
> you. (Ps. 86:5)

I have discovered that far too many people find this hard to
grasp. God is the author of mercy. *God is love!* (1 John 4:8).
Why is it so hard for so many of us to believe that God would
desire to demonstrate his tenderness and kindness when dealing with us?

[The LORD] who redeems your life from the pit,
    who crowns you with steadfast love and
mercy. . . .
The LORD is merciful and gracious,
    slow to anger and abounding in steadfast love.
He will not always chide,
    nor will he keep his anger forever.
He does not deal with us according to our sins,
    nor repay us according to our iniquities.
For as high as the heavens are above the earth,
    so great is his steadfast love toward those who
fear him;
as far as the east is from the west,
    so far does he remove our transgressions from us.
(Ps. 103:4, 8–12)

The LORD is gracious and merciful,
    slow to anger and abounding in steadfast love.
The LORD is good to all,
    and his mercy is over all that he has made. . . .
The LORD is righteous in all his ways
    and kind in all his works.
The LORD is near to all who call on him,
    to all who call on him in truth.
He fulfills the desire of those who fear him;
    he also hears their cry and saves them.
(Ps. 145:8–9, 17–19)

"Rend your hearts and not your garments."
    Return to the LORD your God,

for he is gracious and merciful,
    slow to anger, and abounding in steadfast love;
and he relents over disaster.
    Who knows whether he will not turn and relent,
and leave a blessing behind him,
    a grain offering and a drink offering
for the LORD your God? (Joel 2:13–14)

The steadfast love of the LORD never ceases;
    his mercies never come to an end;
they are new every morning;
    great is your faithfulness.
For the Lord will not
    cast off forever,
but, though he cause grief, he will have compassion
    according to the abundance of his steadfast love.
(Lam. 3:22–23, 31–32)

But God, being rich in mercy, because of the great
love with which he loved us, even when we were
dead in our trespasses, made us alive together with
Christ—by grace you have been saved. (Eph. 2:4–5)

When we ask, God forgives. He is our patient Savior. God longs to show his goodness and his tender kindness toward us. He chooses not to harbor anger. God hears our cries. He redeems us.

Each morning he finds new ways to demonstrate his compassion for us. He is always good, always loving, always faithful, and always compassionate toward us. God's commitment is ferocious. His love for us is unfailing. He allows us to face tough times, but he promises to never leave us. And because of his great love, he has redeemed us. God proved his love and mercy by sending Jesus to die on our behalf. He has adopted us into his family.

God is your Abba and you are his child!

Endnotes

1. Mark Brumley, "Why God is Father and Not Mother," ETNW: Global Catholic Network, accessed February 23, 2013, http://www.ewtn.com/library/Theology/NOTMOTHR.HTM.

2. J. I. Packer, *Knowing God* (Westmont, Illinois: InterVarsity Press, 1973), 201–202.

3. "God is Easy to Live With," Last Days Ministries, accessed February 23, 2013, http://www.lastdaysministries.org/Groups/1000087838/Last_Days_Ministries/Articles/Other_Authors/God_Is_Easy/God_Is_Easy.aspx.

4. Benjamin Hanbury, *Historical Memorials Relating to the Independents or Congregationalists: Volume III* (London: Fisher, Son, & Co., 1844), 537.

5. Merriam-Webster, Inc., "Vouchsafe – Definition and More from Free Merriam-Webster Dictionary," accessed January 1, 2014, http://www.merriam-webster.com/dictionary/vouchsafe.

6.Charles Spurgeon, "The Fatherhood of God," *Essential Works of Charles Spurgeon* (Uhrichsville, OH: Barbour Publishing, 2009).

7. Sam Storms, "God's Passionate Love," *Charisma Magazine*, August 24, 2011, accessed November 15, 2013, http://www.charismamag.com/site-archives/610-spiritled-woman/spiritled-woman/14397-gods-passionate-love.

8. Sowing Circle, Inc., *Blue Letter Bible*, "Greek Lexicon::G5 (KJV)," accessed January 1, 2014, http://www.blueletterbible.org/lang/lexicon/lexicon.cfm?Strongs=G5&t=KJV

9. Brennan Manning, *Abba's Child: The Cry of the Heart for Intimate Belonging with Bonus Content [Kindle Edition]* (Colorado Springs: NavPress, 2012).

10. Ibid.

Chapter 7

Pardon versus Justification

Alfred Dreyfus was a Jewish artillery officer in the army of France. In 1894, Dreyfus was accused of selling secrets to the enemies of France and was arrested on the charges of treason and espionage. This case was one of the most notorious political dramas of the nineteenth century and one of the most notable in modern European history.[1]

Dreyfus was tried in a secret court-martial, convicted of being a traitor, publicly stripped of his army rank, and condemned to the French penal colony on Devil's Island—one of the most infamous prisons in human history. The friends of

Dreyfus were unsatisfied with the trial. They believed it had been rigged and prejudiced against Dreyfus, simply because he was Jewish. Due to his friends' avid protests, as well as those of several members of the French press, Dreyfus was granted a second trial in 1899. However, Dreyfus was again found guilty. This time the public dissatisfaction with the trial caused such a protest and such an outcry that the president of France granted Dreyfus a *pardon*. In the eyes of the law he was still guilty, but he was no longer expected to pay the price for his guilt.

Dreyfus was released from Devil's Island and permitted to go home. However, the stigma of being a traitor still rested on Dreyfus. He had been disgraced publicly. Very few people in France would befriend him. He soon realized the French press who had so vigilantly defended him had simply used his case to advance their self-serving ambitions. Dreyfus was unable to get a job, had lost his pension as a military member, and he had a very difficult time getting any kind of formal education.

But in 1906, a third trial was held for Dreyfus. This time, a fair military commission presided over the trial. Dreyfus was found not guilty. After twelve years of carrying the burden of being labeled a traitor, he was finally fully exonerated and his record completely overturned. He was declared *righteous* in the eyes of the law.[2]

Dreyfus was no longer merely pardoned, but now he had been fully *justified*. Dreyfus was immediately reinstated into the French military. Prior to his arrest, he had served as a low-level artillery officer; but now, he was promoted to the rank of Major and was awarded the French Legion of Honor, which was the highest honor given in all of France.

"The Dreyfus Affair," as it was called in France, illustrates the key differences between a pardon and full justification. Far too many Christians see God's salvific work as a mere pardon rather than what it truly is—*complete justification!*

A pardon says that you are certainly guilty but the penalty of guilt is suspended. You are no longer expected to pay the price that you rightfully owe. However, justification is very different. Justification declares you innocent of any wrongdoing. As previously mentioned, my pastor back in Philadelphia explained justification in these words: "Justified means 'just-as-if' it never happened." Pardon is the removal of the condemnation that you so appropriately deserve, but justification is the act of God wherein he bestows the merits of Christ's record to you. Pardon is an act of mercy. Justification is an act of grace.

Justification is vital to your emotional and spiritual well-being. It is essential that you fully understand and embrace the fact that you are not merely pardoned, but fully justified!

What Is Justification?

The separation between you and God before Christ enters your life is a grand chasm that cannot possibly be overstated. Justification is the bridge by which you can close that insurmountable gap. *The architect of the bridge is God the Father, the cornerstone of the bridge is Jesus Christ, and your guide along the way is the Holy Spirit.* The only way you can actually cross this bridge is by simple and genuine belief in Christ.

According to dictionary.com, "justified" means "to declare innocent or guiltless; to absolve; to acquit; to declare free of blame."[3] The biblical word for "justify" comes from the Greek

> Justification is instantaneously complete upon conversion. If you are a sincere follower of Christ, then you have been fully justified.

word *dikaioō*. This word does not mean "to pardon" or "to forgive," but literally means to declare righteous in a judicial sense.[4] Justification refers to being found completely *not guilty* in a court of law.

When you put your faith in Jesus Christ, you are converted—converted from death to life, from being an enemy of God to now being a friend of God. This conversion takes place by way of judicial decree. God, the Supreme Judge, lays down the verdict. He declares that you are not guilty, that you are righteous. And it is he who proclaims to all of heaven that you are just as righteous as his own Son. This is justification. This is the gospel!

Justification is instantaneously complete upon conversion. If you are a sincere follower of Christ, then you have been fully justified. You will never be any more justified than you are right now, nor will you ever be any less justified. One of the best and simplest comments I have ever read on justification came from the nineteenth-century attorney, politician, and lay preacher William Plumer:

> Justification is an ACT. It is not a work, or a series of acts. It is not progressive. The weakest believer and the strongest saint are alike and equally justified. Justification admits no degrees. A man is either wholly justified or wholly condemned in the sight of God.[5]

Justification is a transcendent truth that must be brazenly defended and intimately embraced by each believer. It is only by thoroughly understanding the doctrine of justification that you can fully enjoy the grace that God has bestowed upon you. Understanding justification is intrinsically woven together with experiencing the abundant life that God desires for you.

There are many doctrines taught throughout Scripture and all of them are important, but I cannot find any truth of the Bible more essential to the peace and rest of the believer than justification. It was the study and understanding of justification that sparked and fueled the Reformation of the sixteenth century. And today, by understanding this precious doctrine, you can spark and fuel a personal reformation in your own heart and life—if one is needed.

We Have Been Justified

Forgiveness is wonderful, pardon is great, and the supernatural cleansing of our souls is certainly magnificent, but to be justified is even more wonderful! Justification, along with imputed righteousness, is the essence of the gospel message. Very few truths are more cardinal to our Christian faith. Pastor and author John Piper says this:

> I have watched this doctrine of justification
> ignite both storms of controversy and great
> awakenings. . . . So, with a passion for reformation
> and revival, I long to see this precious truth of the
> imputed righteousness of Christ defended, known,
> and embraced.[6]

We are all guilty of breaking God's Law. No matter how hard we might try to obey, in the end we will break it. God's Law is not capable of declaring us righteous because we are incapable of obeying it perfectly. Instead, God made a way for us to be completely justified and declared righteous by belief in Christ:

> Let it be known to you therefore, brothers, that
> through this man forgiveness of sins is proclaimed to
> you, and by him everyone who believes is freed from
> everything from which you could not be freed by the
> law of Moses. (Acts 13:38–39)

We have been fully justified from everything that we could not be justified from through our own works. They are powerless to eradicate our sins. It is only by our faith in Christ that we can be justified.

The misunderstanding of justification appears to be the foundation of almost all erroneous theology—contemporary and historical. Martin Luther wrote,

> All heretics have continually failed in this one point,
> that they do not rightly understand or know the
> article of justification.[7]

I have heard preachers say things like, "We're guilty, but Jesus paid the penalty." That is not precise truth; that is incomplete. Before we place our faith in Christ, we are declared guilty, but after we place our faith in Christ, we are no longer considered guilty at all. The complete truth is that we are not guilty at all, because Jesus paid the penalty!

Once you have been justified, you are no longer guilty. We are completely exonerated! It is as if we were able to go back in time and erase the events of the past, as if they never even happened at all. The slate has been wiped clean. Consider these Scriptures:

> I, I am he
>> who blots out your transgressions for
> my own sake,
>> and I will not remember your sins.
> (Isa. 43:25)

> He will again have compassion on us;
>> he will tread our iniquities underfoot.
> You will cast all our sins
>> into the depths of the sea. (Mic. 7:19)

> He has now reconciled in his body of flesh by his death, in order to present you holy and blameless and above reproach before him, if indeed you continue in the faith, steady and steadfast. (Col. 1:22–23)

The misunderstanding of justification appears to be the foundation of almost all erroneous theology.

God does not want our past to be held against us in any way, shape, or form. We are free from accusations. Australian theologian Leon Morris explained justification:

> The righteousness we have is not our own, it comes as God's good gift in Christ. But we will be righteous. Notice that this means more than being pardoned. The pardoned criminal bears no penalty, but he bears a stigma. He is a criminal and he is known as a criminal, albeit an unpunished one. The justified sinner not only bears no penalty; he is righteous. He is not a man with his sins still about him.[8]

God has fully expunged all of our sins from the record book—past, present, and future! *God has erased our sin and our failures from the history books. Our history is made new. Our record is completely wiped clean.* God has chosen to forget our old records. He does not remember them, not because he is unable to remember—surely God is *not* some absentminded old fool—but because he has chosen to forget:

> And you . . . God made alive together with him,
> having forgiven us all our trespasses, by canceling the
> record of debt that stood against us with its legal
> demands. This he set aside, nailing it to the cross. He
> disarmed the rulers and authorities and put them to
> open shame, by triumphing over them in him.
> (Col. 2:13–15)

Here the Apostle Paul explains how Christ triumphed over the curse that condemned us prior to our justification. God makes a mockery of those evil principalities that would seek to prosecute us (a.k.a. Satan and his goon squad). On several occasions, Paul wrote emphatically about the freedom that comes from understanding and embracing freedom that comes from justification by faith alone. One such occurrence was in his letter to the Galatians. Many of these Christians, converted to Christ during Paul's first missionary journey, began to depend on their performance to achieve justification. Paul believed this to be an incredible perversion of

> God has fully expunged all of our sins from the record book—past, present, and future!

the truth. He caught wind of what was happening in Galatia and he responded sharply:

> I am astonished that you are so quickly deserting him
> who called you in the grace of Christ and are turning
> to a different gospel—not that there is another one,
> but there are some who trouble you and want to
> distort the gospel of Christ. (Gal. 1:6–7)

As you read through the book of Galatians, it is clear that Paul was extremely frustrated with the Christians of Galatia, specifically with the fact that they had abandoned the freedom that God had set forth for them. Paul made it clear that being bound by obligation to do the right things is not a gospel—not good news at all. *Paul wanted them to understand they were not just merely pardoned, but they were fully justified.* It is understanding justification that brings freedom.

Justification by Faith Alone

Justification is intrinsically woven together with the imputation of righteousness. Both doctrines are at the very heart of the message of the New Testament. And, like the imputation of righteousness, justification is only triggered in our lives by simple belief, not behavior. We are justified only by genuine faith in Christ.

> *It will be counted to us who believe* in him who raised
> from the dead Jesus our Lord, who was delivered up
> for our trespasses and raised for our justification.

Therefore, since we have been justified by faith,
we have peace with God through our Lord Jesus
Christ. (Rom. 4:24–5:1, emphasis mine)

Yet we know that a person is not justified by works of
the law but through faith in Jesus Christ, so we also
have believed in Christ Jesus, in order to be *justified
by faith in Christ and not by works of the law,* because
by works of the law no one will be justified. . . .

So then, the law was our guardian until Christ
came, in order that we might be justified by faith.
(Gal. 2:16; 3:24, emphasis mine)

To those who have obtained a faith of equal standing
with ours by the righteousness of our God and Savior
Jesus Christ:

May grace and peace be multiplied to you
in the knowledge of God and of Jesus our Lord.
(2 Pet. 1:1–2)

Justification is received by belief, not behavior, bringing us to
know and love God more. *Justification by faith alone is the very
essence of the gospel message!*

For while we were still weak, at the right time Christ
died for the ungodly. For one will scarcely die for a
righteous person—though perhaps for a good person
one would dare even to die—but God shows his love
for us in that while we were still sinners, Christ died
for us. *Since, therefore, we have now been justified by*

his blood, much more shall we be saved by him from the wrath of God. For if while we were enemies we were reconciled to God by the death of his Son, much more, now that we are reconciled, shall we be saved by his life. (Rom. 5:6–10, emphasis mine)

In his preaching and teaching on this passage, pastor and author Matt Chandler recently said these simple but powerful words:

The word justified means that you and I stand before God acceptable, spotless, pure, and without sin. God looks at us and says, 'There is no sin in that man! There is no sin in that woman!' All that blasphemy that we've done by choosing stuff over God; all the blasphemy we've lived in by saying, 'My way is better than God's.' All the blatant sin of saying, 'Creation is better than God' is REMOVED and God sees us as just. . . . This is GREAT NEWS! There's nothing about your effort in that text at all; Nothing about your might, your religious stamina, your morality. . . . You have been justified by an act of God![9]

More than a century before Matt Chandler preached on justification, Charles Spurgeon was building his preaching reputation on the doctrine of justification, and often preached with poignant words on the topic:

I do not believe we can preach the gospel, if we do not preach justification by faith, without works; nor unless we preach the sovereignty of God in

His dispensation of grace; nor unless we exalt
the electing, unchangeable, eternal, immutable,
conquering love of Jehovah.[10]

We cannot preach the gospel message accurately unless we are preaching justification by faith alone. It is that simple! Justification is the gospel.

We have been freed from the spiritual tyranny of guilt. This is an amazing freedom! In his paraphrase of Romans 8:1–3, Eugene Peterson gives us a thrilling depiction of the freedom from condemnation we now have in Christ:

> With the arrival of Jesus, the Messiah, that fateful
> dilemma is resolved. Those who enter into Christ's
> being-here-for-us no longer have to live under a
> continuous, low-lying black cloud. A new power is
> in operation. The Spirit of life in Christ, like a strong
> wind, has magnificently cleared the air, freeing you
> from a fated lifetime of brutal tyranny at the hands of
> sin and death.
>
>   God went for the jugular when he sent his own
> Son. He didn't deal with the problem as something
> remote and unimportant. In his Son, Jesus, he
> personally took on the human condition, entered the
> disordered mess of struggling humanity in order to
> set it right once and for all. (MSG)

We have been declared righteous—fully justified by our faith in Christ—and as such, we never have to walk around with that proverbial "low-lying black cloud" hanging over our heads.

God "went for the jugular." He finished the job. We have no reason to ever feel guilty. Once you have been justified, God no longer sees your failures or transgressions. God the Father only sees the righteousness of his own Son with which you have been clothed:

> I will greatly rejoice in the LORD;
>> my soul shall exult in my God,
> for he has clothed me with the garments of salvation;
>> he has covered me with the robe of righteousness.
> (Isa. 61:10)

So many Christians allow their minds to be monopolized by guilt and shame. Guilt and shame are cancers destroying our souls, devouring our ability to be lovingly embraced by the Father, and shattering our confidence. Instead of having your mind preoccupied with your failures, you must choose to believe that your record of failures has been eradicated. Celebrate the fact that God has pronounced (in front of all of heaven) that you are in right standing. Choose to believe that you have been justified.

Whenever you have these negative thoughts and emotions, quote the Scriptures aloud and ask God to give you the ability to choose to believe his Word over your bad thinking.

Many Christians feel *dirty* and assume that whatever they feel about themselves is exactly what God must see when he looks down at us. We cannot earn this gift of righteousness. It is only by grace. It is because of our faith (not anything we do) that the Father has chosen to justify us. He has given us this mind-blowing gift of righteousness . . . a free gift! And let me

159

make this clear, when I say "free," I do not mean to imply that it is cheap. This gift is free to us through faith, but it is only made available to us after the most expensive purchase ever made in all of human history. Christ paid a great price so that we might be justified.

The Apostle Paul reminded one of his protégés that it is only through Christ that we have been forgiven, made clean, justified, and declared righteous:

> Jesus Christ, who gave himself for us to redeem us from all lawlessness and to purify for himself a people for his own possession who are zealous for good works. . . .
>
> He saved us, not because of works done by us in righteousness, but according to his own mercy, by the washing of regeneration and renewal of the Holy Spirit, whom he poured out on us richly through Jesus Christ our Savior, so that being justified by his grace we might become heirs according to the hope of eternal life. (Tit. 2:13–14; 3:5–7)

I have often seen believers subconsciously driven by a constant desire to try to *earn* God's grace, wrestling with their need to make themselves inwardly feel worthy. Too many forget that we cannot earn the grace of God. We can only embrace and celebrate what God has chosen to do for us. We could never achieve righteousness or justification. Christ made it possible for us to be declared righteous:

And the free gift is not like the result of that one
man's sin. For the judgment following one trespass
brought condemnation, *but the free gift following
many trespasses brought justification.* For if, because
of one man's trespass, death reigned through that
one man, much more will those who receive *the
abundance of grace and the free gift of righteousness*
reign in life through the one man Jesus Christ.

Therefore, as one trespass led to condemnation
for all men, *so one act of righteousness leads to
justification* and life for all men. (Rom. 5:16–18,
emphasis mine)

We have nothing to be ashamed of. We have nothing to feel
guilty about. If we had merely been pardoned, then maybe we
would deserve the stigma that follows a pardoned criminal;
but we are not merely pardoned. We have been fully justified
. . . just as if we had never broken God's Law in the first place.
*No more scarlet letter on your blouse; no more record of your
failures.*

The life of the believer can truly be revolutionized if he
genuinely understands and chooses to embraces the doctrine
of justification by faith alone. It is this truth of justification
that relieves our sense of the nagging embarrassment when
we believe that God is angry with us or disappointed in us. It is
when we truly understand that our sin records have been erased
that great confidence is birthed within us. Our knowledge of

justification comforts us in times of failure and despair. John Piper puts it this way:

> There is so much brokenness and so much sin that
> seems intransigently woven together with forms of
> failing family life and distorted personal perspectives.
> This does not yield to quick remedies. After several
> decades of watching the mental health care system
> at work, I am less hopeful about the effectiveness of
> even Christian psychotherapy than I used to be. . . .
> But more than ever I believe the essential foundation
> of all healing and all Christ-exalting wholeness is
> a soul-penetrating grasp of the glorious truth of
> justification by faith.[11]

Understanding the doctrine of justification can and will transform the heart and mind of the believer. The doctrine of justification by faith cannot be taught too much or too often. Charles Spurgeon put it this way:

> I think, dear friends, some of you will be saying,
> "There is that same old doctrine again that we are
> so continually hearing," and I am sure if you do say
> it I shall not be surprised. Nor, on the other hand,
> shall I make any sort of excuse. The Doctrine of
> Justification by Faith through the substitutionary
> Sacrifice of Christ is very much to my ministry what
> bread and salt are to the table. As often as ever the
> table is set, there are those necessary things. I regard
> that Doctrine as being one that is to be preached

continually, to be mixed up with all our sermons. . . . Indeed, it is impossible to bring it forward too often. It is the soul-saving Doctrine—it is the foundation Doctrine of the Gospel of Jesus Christ![12]

> Justification is the doctrine by which the church stands or falls.

Justification Equals Revival

There is no truth in Scripture that will inspire revival as fast as the doctrine of justification. Digesting and embracing this truth always has the same effect on believers—simply put, a greater desire to worship God! That is why it is so essential that we boldly teach and defend this precious doctrine!

It was by studying and understanding this doctrine that a revolution was started in the heart of Martin Luther, and eventually brought about the Reformation. The church corporately embraced justification, which brought great revival to the entire continent of Europe and eventually to the entire known world. Justification inspires worship, prayer, and holy living faster than any other doctrine. If you are a pastor wanting to see revival in your church, teach justification boldly and often. Mighty things will start happening.

Sixteenth-century theologian Philipp Melanchthon referred to the doctrine of justification as "the chief article of the Gospel," and he challenged the church to make justification the most important "topic of Christian doctrine."[13]

Justification is the doctrine by which the church stands or falls. It is essential for preachers to properly present and boldly teach this doctrine. Many contemporary Bible teachers have ignored these precious doctrines. This, however, is not only a new phenomenon. The church has been dealing with this for a while.

The prominent nineteenth-century author and theologian A. W. Pink often preached about the imputation of righteousness and justification by faith alone. Nearly a century ago, he wrote about how many churches have neglected these precious doctrines:

> This is, perhaps, the most wonderful of all the "results" obtained by the arduous Work of our blessed Savior. Yet is it today, in most professing Christian circles, the least understood. If it be true that the blessed truths of reconciliation, remission and redemption have been grievously and grossly misrepresented by many who have posed as teachers sent from God, that which is now to be before us has been flatly denied, held up to ridicule, and branded as a serious error. . . .
>
> But today that inestimably blessed truth which we now desire to set before the reader (as the Lord is pleased to enable), is not so much denied, as it is *ignored*. That which is the crowning glory of the Gospel (Rom 1:17), that by which God has supremely displayed His infinite wisdom (1Co 2:7), that which should most of all render the Redeemer precious to His people (Psa 71:14–16), and that which ought to be the chief object of the believer's joy (Isa 61:10), is now left out of almost all so-called evangelical ministry.

Even where Christ is presented as the sinner's only hope, and His blood as the only cleanser of sin, that which secures a title for Heaven, that which alone can render a sinner acceptable before the Judge of all the earth, that which is the ground upon which He pronounces the ungodly *justified*, is missing from the best preaching and writings of this degenerate age. At best, only a half Gospel is being proclaimed, only the negative side of what Christ earned for His people is being set before them.[14]

The same problems Pink observed in the latter stages of the nineteenth century are the same problems we observe today in the twenty-first century. Many preachers are only preaching one side of what Christ did at the cross—the forgiveness of sin, often taught as a mere judicial pardon. But the wondrous work of the cross accomplished much more than just a pardon. Justification!

Why is this so essential to your spiritual well-being? Understanding that I have been fully justified and declared righteous, no matter what I do or no matter how many times I fail, sustains me through all my failures, through all my sins, and through my many stupid choices. Knowing that I have been justified brings tremendous freedom for me to enjoy God's plans, without the worries that my failures and sins will separate me from Him. If we are to ever see mass revival and reformation in the church today, we must boldly proclaim and fiercely defend the doctrine of justification, just as the Reformers did nearly five hundred years ago. *Justification by faith alone is absolutely the right and proper biblical view of justification, not just the historic Reformed Protestant view.*

Our sins should have led to our eternal punishment, but God's gift has made it possible for us to be made righteous. We have been fully justified. We are considered blameless and righteous, whether we sin a little or sin a lot—it makes no difference! Pink put it this way:

> The justification of the Christian is complete the moment he truly believes in Christ, and hence there are no degrees in justification. The Apostle Paul was as truly a justified man at the hour of his conversion as he was at the close of his life. The feeblest babe in Christ is just as completely justified as is the most mature saint.[15]

We have been forgiven of our sins, but we have also been fully justified by faith alone, imputed with the righteousness of God, and invited into his royal family.

Endnotes

1. "Alfred Dreyfus (French military officer)—Encyclopedia Britannica," Encyclopedia Britannica, Inc., accessed June 23, 2012, http://www.britannica.com/EBchecked/topic/171509/Alfred-Dreyfus.

2. "Dreyfus affair (French history)—Encyclopedia Britannica," Encyclopedia Britannica, Inc., accessed June 23, 2012, http://www.britannica.com/EBchecked/topic/171538/Dreyfus-affair.

3. Dictionary.com, LLC, "Justified | Define Justified at Dictionary.com," accessed February 9, 2013, http://dictionary.reference.com/browse/justified?s=t.

4. Sowing Circle, Inc., *Blue Letter Bible*, "Greek Lexicon::G1344 (ĸᴊv)," accessed February 13, 2013, http://www.blueletterbible.org/lang/lexicon/lexicon.cfm?Strongs=G1344&t=KJV.

5. William S. Plumer, *The Grace of Christ, or Sinners Saved by Unmerited Kindness* (Philadelphia: Presbyterian Board of Publication, 1853), 195.

6. "Crossway Books Interview with John Piper on Counted Righteous in Christ," Desiring God, March 20, 2003, accessed February 23, 2013, http://www.desiringgod.org/resource-library/interviews/crossway-books-interview-with-john-piper-on-counted-righteous-in-christ.

7. Martin Luther, quoted in John B. Alden, *The Library Magazine,* vol. 3 (New York, New Jersy: John B. Alden Publisher, 1887), 256.

8. Leon Morris, *The Cross in the New Testament* (Grand Rapids: Eerdmans, 1965), 247.

9. Matt Chandler, quoted in "Why Jesus?" Authentic Manhood, accessed November 10, 2013, http://www.authenticmanhood.com/why-jesus.

10. Charles Spurgeon, "A Defense of Calvinism," The Spurgeon Archive, accessed February 12, 2013, http://www.spurgeon.org/calvinis.htm.

11. John Piper and Justin Taylor, "What God Requires, Christ Provides," Desiring God, January 1, 2004, accessed November 10, 2013, http://www.desiringgod.org/resource-library/articles/what-god-requires-christ-provides.

12. Charles Spurgeon, "Justification, Propitiation, Declaration," Christian Classics Ethereal Library, originally published December 2, 1915, accessed November 10, 2013, http://www.ccel.org/ccel/spurgeon/sermons61.xlix.html.

13. "Augsburgh Confession," *The Book of Concord: The Confessions of the Lutheran Church*, Bookofconcord.org, accessed January 1, 2014, http://bookofconcord.org/augsburgconfession.php.

14. A. W. Pink, quoted in "The Satisfaction of Christ Studies in the Atonement" (Swengel, Pennsylvania: Biblical Truth Depot, 1955), accessed February 23, 2013, http://www.pbministries.org/books/pink/Satisfaction/sat_16.htm.

15. A. W. Pink, *The Doctrine of Justification* (Public domain), 50, http://www.ntslibrary.com/PDF%20Books%20II/The%20Doctrine%20of%20Justification%20-%20Pink.pdf.

Chapter 8

Citizenship and Divine Rights

Bruce Willis is one of my all-time favorite actors. He was fantastic as Detective John McClane in the classic *Die Hard* series, and even better as Dr. Malcolm Crowe in *The Sixth Sense*. However, it's one of his lesser known films that most grabbed my heart. *Tears of the Sun* is about a team of Navy SEALS led by Bruce Willis's character Lieutenant A. K. Waters. The nation of Nigeria collapses and is taken over by a ruthless military dictator. The United States government senses that an American missionary doctor living in a remote

Nigerian village is in danger. Lieutenant Waters and his elite team are dispatched to rescue the doctor.

The Navy SEALs are the greatest special operations task force ever created. They are tactically far superior to any other Special Forces team. Their focus is reconnaissance operations, hostage rescue, unconventional warfare, and counter-terrorism. The Navy SEALs are the *best of the best*. The doctor's citizenship merited a team of our nation's best. They were sent to save her and to protect her at the risk of their own lives. She deserved this incredible protection and service, as do all United States citizens, because of her status as a citizen. Citizenship merits and guarantees certain several exceptional benefits: protection, liberty, defense, and support.

Well, the same in true in the kingdom of God. We are citizens of heaven, and our citizenship is what merits our right to certain promises and provisions guaranteed in the Word of God:

> But our citizenship is in heaven, and from it we await a Savior, the Lord Jesus Christ, who will transform our lowly body to be like his glorious body, by the power that enables him even to subject all things to himself. (Phil. 3:20–21)

> For through him we both have access in one Spirit to the Father. So then you are no longer strangers and aliens, but you are fellow citizens with the saints and members of the household of God, built on the foundation of the apostles and prophets, Christ Jesus himself being the cornerstone. (Eph. 2:18–20)

God sent his own Navy SEAL team to rescue us, to ensure our freedom. Nearly two thousand years ago, a brave man died for us. God did not send a second-tier rescue team. He sent his absolute best—the best of the best—his very own Son, Jesus Christ.

> God did not send a second-tier rescue team. He sent his absolute best—the best of the best—his very own Son, Jesus Christ.

We Are Citizens of Heaven

As a citizen of heaven you are entitled to whatever the King has declared and ordained for you. Some Christians are uncomfortable with the word "entitled." But I contend this is exactly the right vernacular to use. We have not earned our rights as citizens (that has been accomplished for us by Christ at the cross), but we most certainly are entitled.

As citizens of the magnificent kingdom of heaven, we have been given the right to share in the inheritance promised to all the people who love God. Consider these words from the Apostle Paul:

> Giving thanks to the Father, who has qualified you to share in the inheritance of the saints in light. He has delivered us from the domain of darkness and transferred us to the kingdom of his beloved Son. (Col. 1:12–13)

You are a citizen in God's kingdom, elevated to the highest possible status within that kingdom. Your performance or behavior does not affect your status with God. Just like your righteousness cannot be negated by your behavior, your

> Righteousness is God's stamp of approval on you.

citizenship cannot be negated either. Even if we fail, even if we don't pray enough, even if we allow our old sinful habits to creep back into our lives, nothing negates your citizenship in God's kingdom. Whether you are a *good Christian* or not is irrelevant.

As human beings, we will sometimes make bad choices. As such, we will often have to face the consequences of our choices here on earth, or we may end up suffering from some self-inflicted pain, but even while we face the natural consequences of our actions, God still remains faithful to us. He does not nullify our citizenship when we blow it.

You Have the Divine Right to Blessings

At the exact moment of your belief, you inherited a whole heap of promises and protections. Don't take what the Bible says about your inheritance lightly. Righteousness is far more than just a fancy theological term. Righteousness is God's stamp of approval on you. Understanding that approval is the master key to receiving the inheritance God has ordained for you.

This begs the question, what are the blessings I have been promised? The one promise that immediately stands out is the promise of *abundant life*. Jesus Christ said these powerful words:

> The thief comes only to steal and kill and destroy. I came that they may have life and have it abundantly. (John 10:10)

The word for "abundantly" here is translated from the Greek word *perissos*. This word can mean "superfluous," "overflowing," or "over and above a certain quantity."[1] God is promising us a life "overflowing." I can only attempt to imagine the great potential God has endowed me with. The Apostle Paul penned these words to the church at Corinth:

> But, as it is written,
>
>> "What no eye has seen, nor ear heard,
>>> nor the heart of man imagined,
>> what God has prepared for those who love him"—
>
> these things God has revealed to us through the Spirit. For the Spirit searches everything, even the depths of God. For who knows a person's thoughts except the spirit of that person, which is in him? So also no one comprehends the thoughts of God except the Spirit of God. Now we have received not the spirit of the world, but the Spirit who is from God, that we might understand the things freely given us by God. (1 Cor. 2:9–12)

Of course Paul is not writing a new idea here, he is actually quoting from the Old Testament Scriptures. It was a common theme amongst Old Testament writers to proclaim their confidence in God's ability and willingness to work together great plans for his people. God deeply cares for each one of us. *He has great plans for us. Incredible plans!* The prophet Jeremiah said these well known words:

> For I know the plans I have for you, declares the
> LORD, plans for welfare and not for evil, to give you a
> future and a hope. (Jer. 29:11)

By his divine providence, God has orchestrated our lives to abundantly overflow with the blessings promised to us in his Word. You are entitled to live out the great plans he has in store for you. God longs for you to fulfill these great plans, bringing him great glory and honor. And God has promised to bless those he has declared righteous.

> *For you bless the righteous, O LORD*;
> you cover him with favor as with a shield. (Ps. 5:12)

There are literally hundreds of scriptures in which God has promised to protect us, provide for us, and bless us. Though everything is not going to be perfect with our lives, God's divine hand will be there. Tough times will certainly come our way, but God has promised to work everything out for our good:

> And we know that for those who love God all things
> work together for good, for those who are called
> according to his purpose. (Rom. 8:28)

Jesus also told us that we would have hard times, but he also proclaimed that our lives ought to stand out as different in the midst of any such troubles:

> I have said these things to you, that in me you may
> have peace. In the world you will have tribulation.

But take heart; I have overcome the world.
(John 16:33)

God wants you to walk in confidence, knowing that he is with you and that he is in favor of you. God is your protection. John Piper wrote these encouraging words:

> The world will bring its condemnation. They may even put the sword behind it. But we know that the highest court has already ruled in our favor. . . . If they reject us, he accepts us. If they hate us, he loves us. If they imprison us, he sets our spirits free. If they afflict us, he refines us by the fire. If they kill us, he makes a passage to paradise. They cannot defeat us. Christ has died. Christ is risen. We are alive in him. And in him there is no condemnation. We are forgiven, and we are righteous. "And the righteous are as bold as a lion." (Prov. 28:1)[2]

God desires that we be filled with courage and confidence in him. He desires our lives to be overflowing with joy no matter what dilemmas or trials come our way. God has already blessed us tremendously in so many ways, more than what we could ever even realize. And we can always be confident that he will continue to bless:

> Blessed is the one you choose and bring near,
>   to dwell in your courts!
> We shall be satisfied with the goodness of your house,
>   the holiness of your temple! (Ps. 65:4)

"I will feast the soul of the priests with abundance,
    and my people shall be satisfied with my
goodness,
        declares the LORD." (Jer. 31:14)

And from his fullness we have all received, grace upon grace. (John 1:16)

Blessed be the God and Father of our Lord Jesus Christ, who has blessed us in Christ with every spiritual blessing in the heavenly places. (Eph. 1:3)

Every good gift and every perfect gift is from above, coming down from the Father of lights with whom there is no variation or shadow due to change. (James 1:17)

Your Blessings Have a Purpose

God has rescued and redefined me so that I could have friendship with him. This is between God and me. I am free to enjoy his love. But God doesn't stop there. He doesn't just want it to remain between him and me. God has promised me all sorts of blessings and provisions, but they are not just for my own satisfaction in him, but for several greater purposes as well.

We have certain rights and protections and provisions promised to us as citizens of heaven, and these promises have a purpose. Why would God want us to have these blessings? The answer is really quite simple . . . so that God might glorify himself through us!

God can bring tremendous glory back unto himself through the lives of people who live abundantly in his name. God certainly does not need me to bring glory to his name. He is more than capable of accomplishing that task on his own. However, it does seem to me that God's favorite way of glorifying himself is through the lives of the people he has already redefined.

> God is writing his story in the lives of other people, and he is inviting each one of us to be a part of the story-writing.

God is writing his story in the lives of other people, and he is inviting each one of us to be a part of the story-writing. We get to be involved in God's work on behalf of others. God has called me to be his ambassador, so that he might rescue others through me (2 Cor. 5:20).

God wants to bless you so that, through your life, he might reveal to others that he is worthy of being worshiped. This has clearly been known to God's people for literally thousands of years. Consider God's covenant with Abram (later Abraham):

> And I will make of you a great nation, and I will bless you and make your name great, so that you will be a blessing. I will bless those who bless you, and him who dishonors you I will curse, and in you all the families of the earth shall be blessed. (Gen. 12:2–3)

God's promise of blessings to Abram was for the purpose of using him to be an instrument of blessing to the rest of the world. The same is true for us. God has provided blessings in our lives to serve a greater purpose and so that we might bless others. In his book *The Treasure Principle*, Randy Alcorn makes this great statement:

> God prospers me not to raise my standard of living but to raise my standard of giving. God gives us more money than we need so we can give—generously.[3]

While Alcorn specifically addresses money, I assert that this applies to all sorts of blessings from God. We have been given resources, wisdom, influence, money, health, material possessions, houses, skills, knowledge, intelligence, friendships, and a whole host of other blessings. God bestows these gifts to us so that we can use them for a greater purpose—*to raise our standard of giving, not just to raise our standard of living.*

That is why I find it particularly odd that some Christians expect God to give all believers great wealth. I am not against acquiring wealth. There is no doubt that God has ordained some to be wealthy. It can be a great tool in spreading the gospel and for doing good works around the world. However, the assumption that every believer should live an extravagant lifestyle and have a boatload of cash is silly.

I've even heard preachers say that a lack of faith is the only thing that will cause a believer not to have great wealth. This line of thinking completely dismisses the sovereignty of God. In response, I would say that God would not want a person to have great wealth if they could not handle it. King Agur seemed to understand this when he prayed this prayer:

> Remove far from me falsehood and lying;
> give me neither poverty nor riches;

> feed me with the food that is needful for me,
> lest I be full and deny you
> and say, "Who is the LORD?"
> or lest I be poor and steal
> and profane the name of my God. (Prov. 30:8–9)

King Agur knew that if he had too little, he would be tempted to live in such a way that he might dishonor God. He also knew that if he had too much, he'd forget his need for God. This prayer demonstrates that we need to always be concerned with honoring God. We would be wise to echo this prayer.

I am not saying that you cannot pray for wealth or influence or resources. Quite the opposite. I encourage you to pray for all such blessings, but you must do so with the right motives. If for some reason you do not end up as a millionaire, that does not necessarily mean that you have missed out on God's best plan for your life or that you did not have enough faith.

You have inherited many promises from God. Because you are imputed with righteousness, you are now in line for blessings. God wants to bless you. If you are a good manager of the blessings God has already given you, he will then entrust you with more (Luke 16:10).

In addition, we ought to be careful to never presume to know exactly what God has allocated for us. God has promised to bless us, but exactly how that unfolds will be different for each believer. Sometimes, we have an idea as to what we believe is best, but remember that God may have something different in mind. Likely something better. *In fact, you can take it to the bank—in the long run, God's plans for you are always better than whatever plans you can conceive for yourself.*

King David seemed to understand this principle. More than two decades before he became king over all of Israel, David demonstrated his confidence in God's blessing when he, against all odds, defeated Goliath. At that time, David was merely a young shepherd boy with no military experience. But he spoke as if he was a warrior—not because of his confidence in himself, but because of his confidence in God. David proclaimed God's promises of protection. He knew that God would protect him as he went into battle against Goliath, but more importantly, David understood the reason why God would protect him in this fight:

> This day the LORD will deliver you into my hand, and I will strike you and take your head from you. And this day I will give the carcasses of the camp of the Philistines to the birds of the air and the wild beasts of the earth, *that all the earth may know that there is a God in Israel.* (1 Sam. 17:46 NKJV, emphasis mine)

David exclaimed that the reason God would step in was so that the whole world would know that "there is a God in Israel." David never lost sight of why God intervened. God's hand of provision and protection is always inspired by God's desire to expand his own glory within humanity.

As I study the life and writings of David, this appears to be a principle constantly in his mind. And I cannot help but sense that this was one of the main reasons why God entrusted David with so much influence, in spite of David's flaws. David's rise to power was not a smooth ride. It was filled with danger, failures, pain, setbacks, heartbreak, and risks. Yet, in the midst of all those things, God was continually faithful to David, mainly because God knew that blessing and protecting David would lead to an expansion of the glory of God to other nations.

We would be wise to be like David in our attitudes. We must never forget the ultimate purpose for the provisions or protections that God bestows upon us. It is all about his love and power being demonstrated through us to the world.

You Are a Royal Priesthood

The comments of the Apostle Peter echo the understanding that David possessed. In his first epistle, Peter exclaimed the wonderful citizenship that we now have, the reason why we have it, and how we ought to respond to the knowledge of such an amazing privilege:

> But you are *a chosen race, a royal priesthood*, a holy nation, a people for his own possession, *that you may proclaim the excellencies of him* who called you out of darkness into his marvelous light. Once you were not a people, *but now you are God's people*; once you had not received mercy, but now you have received mercy.
>
> Beloved, I urge you as sojourners and exiles to abstain from the passions of the flesh, which wage war against your soul. Keep your conduct among the Gentiles honorable, so that when they speak against

you as evildoers, they may see your good deeds and glorify God on the day of visitation. (1 Pet. 2:9–12)

Peter tells us that we have an outstanding new "nationality"—we are "a people for his own possession." Peter also explains why we are so privileged to belong to God: "That you may proclaim the excellencies of him who called you." *There is a clear purpose . . . to proclaim God's excellencies!*

Peter reminds his readers that they are "sojourners and exiles." The King James Version translates this as "strangers and pilgrims," while the New International Version says "aliens and strangers." It is clear: we are not like everyone else around us. We have a citizenship in a different kingdom. We are aliens in this land.

Finally, Peter outlines how we ought to respond to the incredible knowledge of our "royal priesthood." The Apostle tells us to "abstain from the passions of the flesh" and to "keep your conduct among the Gentiles honorable." He also tells us why we ought to respond in this way . . . so that unbelievers who are watching us may "glorify God."

> Far too many Christians miss out on the blessings that God desires to give, simply because too many do not ask.

Again, it is clear that God is blessing us for a greater purpose, not just so that we can enjoy awesome citizenship. God has taken ownership of us so that we can be an example to the world. Yes, our citizenship certainly has tremendous benefits and bonuses, but the primary reason we have this citizenship is so that we can bring glory back to the Father . . . so that we can make him look good.

The knowledge of our citizenship ought to inspire us to endure anything. We ought to be fully satisfied in God and fully satisfied in knowing that we shall spend eternity with him. No matter what troubles or persecution or hardships might come our way, we know we will be with him forever . . . as citizens of his heavenly kingdom.

As unbelievers watch us go through tough times, they ought to be astounded by the joy with which we face any hardship. As the unsaved examine your life from afar (and I can assure you that every unsaved person you know is examining you daily), the joy you have deep within you should compel them to want to serve the same God you serve. God has blessed you, in far more ways than you realize, so that you may reach out to those who are watching you. Your confidence in God's desire to bless you should be so strong that the unsaved people watching you are amazed by the hope inside of you and compelled to inquire about your God.

It's Time to Ask

Far too many Christians miss out on the blessings that God desires to give, simply because too many do not ask. The Apostle Paul tells the church at Philippi, "With thanksgiving let your requests be made known to God" (Phil. 4:6).

James the brother of Jesus addresses the motives of the believer: "You do not have, because you do not ask. You ask and do not receive, because you ask wrongly, to spend it on your passions" (James 4:2–3). The right motive is simply this: seek to make God look good to the rest of the world. If expanding God's kingdom is your top priority, then God will certainly entrust you with resources, influence, finances, and great opportunities. I encourage every believer to petition God with confidence, knowing that he desires to bless us:

> "Therefore I tell you, whatever you ask in prayer, believe that you have received it, and it will be yours." (Mark 11:24)

> "Ask, and it will be given to you; seek, and you will find; knock, and it will be opened to you. For everyone who asks receives, and the one who seeks finds, and to the one who knocks it will be opened. Or which one of you, if his son asks him for bread, will give him a stone? Or if he asks for a fish, will give him a serpent? If you then, who are evil, know how to give good gifts to your children, how much more will your Father who is in heaven give good things to those who ask him!" (Matt. 7:7–11)

In my Bible, these words appear in red; that is, of course, because they came from the mouth of our Lord Jesus. He is teaching us about the importance of asking God for whatever it is we desire. And Jesus tells us that the Father is good, looking for ways to bless us. If we, as evil depraved human beings, know how to bless our own children, then how much more can God bless his children? How much greater will God bless us? Not only *can* he bless us, but we can be certain that he *will* bless us!

You are a citizen of heaven. You can now claim all the promises and blessings set aside for the righteous!

The Many Promises of God

God has allocated a specific inheritance for you.
Your future in Christ is secure, your inheritance
is guaranteed, and his promises will always
remain true!

> God has
> allocated
> a specific
> inheritance
> for you.

Below you will find a compilation of Bible
verses that present just a few of the promises
made to us by God. I ask you to carefully and prayerfully digest
what God is telling us. I know it would be tempting to just
think you'll come back to this some other time, but I request
that you read through this list and think about the guaranteed
blessings and promises that God has dictated for us through
his Word! I also ask that you don't just rush through this list,
as if it's a fast food meal. Take your time, savor and meditate
on each verse, and purposely consider the truth being declared
on your behalf.

The Promise of Joy

> This day is holy to our Lord. And do not be grieved,
> for the joy of the Lord is your strength. (Neh. 8:10)

> You make known to me the path of life;
> in your presence there is fullness of joy;
> at your right hand are pleasures forevermore.
> (Ps 16:11)

> Sing praises to the Lord, O you his saints,
> and give thanks to his holy name.
> For his anger is but for a moment,

and his favor is for a lifetime.
Weeping may tarry for the night,
but joy comes with the morning. (Ps. 30:4–5)

The Promise of Healing

Bless the LORD, O my soul,
and forget not all his benefits,
who forgives all your iniquity,
who heals all your diseases. (Ps. 103:2–3)

For I will restore health to you,
and your wounds I will heal,
declares the LORD. (Jer. 30:17)

He called to him his twelve disciples and gave them
authority over unclean spirits, to cast them out, and
to heal every disease and every affliction. (Matt. 10:1)

And these signs will accompany those who believe: in
my name they will cast out demons; they will speak
in new tongues; they will pick up serpents with their
hands; and if they drink any deadly poison, it will not
hurt them; they will lay their hands on the sick, and
they will recover. (Mark 16:17–18)

Is any one of you sick? He should call the elders of
the church to pray over him and anoint him with the
oil in the name of the Lord. And the prayer offered
in faith will make the sick person well; the Lord will
raise him up. If he has sinned, he will be forgiven.
Therefore confess your sins to each other and pray

for each other so that you may be healed. The prayer
of a righteous man is powerful and effective. (James
5:14–16 NIV)

God's Peace Indwells Us

I will listen to what God the LORD will say;
he promises peace to his people, his saints.
(Ps. 85:8 NIV)

I will heal my people and will let them enjoy
abundant peace and security. (Jer. 33:6 NIV)

The God of peace will soon crush Satan under
your feet. The grace of our Lord Jesus be with you.
(Rom. 16:20)

And the peace of God, which surpasses all
understanding, will guard your hearts and your
minds in Christ Jesus. (Phil. 4:7)

God Promises to Hear Our Prayers

But know that the LORD has set apart the godly for
    himself;
the LORD hears when I call to him. (Ps. 4:3)

The eyes of the LORD are toward the righteous
and his ears toward their cry. . . .
Many are the afflictions of the righteous,
but the LORD delivers him out of them all.
(Ps. 34:15, 19)

So we fasted and petitioned our God about this, and he answered our prayer. (Ezra 8:23 NIV)

Therefore I tell you, whatever you ask in prayer, believe that you have received it, and it will be yours. (Mark 11:24)

And this is the confidence that we have toward him, that if we ask anything according to his will he hears us. (1 John 5:14)

God Is Our Source of Strength

For the eyes of the LORD range throughout the earth to strengthen those whose hearts are fully committed to him. (2 Chron. 16:9 NIV)

The LORD is my strength and my song,
and he has become my salvation;
this is my God, and I will praise him. (Ex. 15:2)

Both riches and honor come from you, and you rule over all. In your hand are power and might, and in your hand it is to make great and to give strength to all. And now we thank you, our God, and praise your glorious name. (1 Chron. 29:12–13)

With him are strength and sound wisdom. (Job 12:16)

For who is God, but the LORD?
And who is a rock, except our God?—

the God who equipped me with strength
and made my way blameless.
He made my feet like the feet of a deer
and set me secure on the heights. (Ps. 18:31–33)

My flesh and my heart may fail,
but God is the strength of my heart and my portion
forever. (Ps. 73:26)

The LORD is my strength and my song;
he has become my salvation.
Glad songs of salvation
are in the tents of the righteous:
"The right hand of the LORD does valiantly."
(Ps. 118:14–15)

On the day I called, you answered me;
my strength of soul you increased. (Ps. 138:3)

O LORD, my Lord, the strength of my salvation,
you have covered my head in the day of battle.
(Ps. 140:7)

If anyone speaks, they should do so as one who
speaks the very words of God. If anyone serves, they
should do so with the strength God provides, so
that in all things God may be praised through Jesus
Christ. To him be the glory and the power for ever
and ever. Amen. (1 Pet. 4:11 NIV)

The LORD is my strength and my shield;
in him my heart trusts, and I am helped;
my heart exults,
and with my song I give thanks to him.

The LORD is the strength of his people;
he is the saving refuge of his anointed. (Ps. 28:7–8)

I can do all things through him who strengthens me.
(Phil. 4:13)

The Promise of Eternal Life

Jesus said to her, "I am the resurrection and the life. Whoever believes in me, though he die, yet shall he live, and everyone who lives and believes in me shall never die." (John 11:25–26)

We were buried therefore with him by baptism into death, in order that, just as Christ was raised from the dead by the glory of the Father, we too might walk in newness of life. (Rom. 6:4)

Behold! I tell you a mystery. We shall not all
sleep, but we shall all be changed, in a moment,
in the twinkling of an eye, at the last trumpet.
For the trumpet will sound, and the dead will be
raised imperishable, and we shall be changed.
(1 Cor. 15:51–52)

God's Comfort and Compassion

The LORD is near to the brokenhearted
and saves the crushed in spirit. (Ps. 34:18)

Your compassion is great O LORD; preserve my life
according to your laws. (Ps. 119:156 NIV)

He heals the brokenhearted
and binds up their wounds. (Ps. 147:3)

As one who his mother comforts,
so I will comfort you. (Isa. 66:13)

Then shall the young women rejoice in the dance,
and the young men and the old shall be merry.
I will turn their mourning into joy;
I will comfort them, and give them gladness for
sorrow. (Jer. 31:13)

Because of the LORD's great love we are not
consumed, for his compassions never fail. They
are new every morning; great is your faithfulness.
(Lam. 3:22–23 NIV)

Blessed be the God and Father of our Lord Jesus
Christ, the Father of mercies and God of all comfort,
who comforts us in all our affliction, so that we may
be able to comfort those who are in any affliction,
with the comfort with which we ourselves are
comforted by God. (2 Cor. 1:3–4)

God's Promise to Always Be Faithful to Us

Yet you have been righteous in all that has come upon
us, for you have dealt faithfully and we have acted
wickedly. (Neh. 9:33)

All the paths of the LORD are steadfast love and
    faithfulness,
for those who keep his covenant and his testimonies.
    (Ps. 25:10)

But you, O Lord, are a God merciful and gracious,
slow to anger and abounding in steadfast love and
faithfulness. (Ps. 86:15)

O LORD God of hosts,
who is mighty as you are, O LORD,
with your faithfulness all around you? (Ps. 89:8)

For your steadfast love is great above the heavens;
your faithfulness reaches to the clouds. (Ps. 108:4)

The saying is trustworthy, for:

If we have died with him, we will also live with him;
if we endure, we will also reign with him;
if we deny him, he also will deny us;
if we are faithless, he remains faithful—

for he cannot deny himself. (2 Tim. 2:11–13)

The Promise of Restoration

> Though who have made me see many troubles, many
> and bitter, you will restore my life again; from the
> depths of the earth you will again bring me up. You
> will increase my honor and comfort me once again.
> (Ps. 71:20–21 NIV)

> I will restore to you the years
> that the swarming locust has eaten,
> the hopper, the destroyer, and the cutter,
> my great army, which I sent among you.

> You shall eat in plenty and be satisfied,
> and praise the name of the LORD your God,
> who has dealt wondrously with you.
> And my people shall never again be put to shame.
> You shall know that I am in the midst of Israel,
> and that I am the LORD your God and there is none else.
> And my people shall never again be put to shame.
> (Joel 2:25–27)

> But now in Christ Jesus you who once were far off
> have been brought near by the blood of Christ.
> (Eph. 2:13)

The Promise of Protection

> But let all who take refuge in you rejoice;
> let them ever sing for joy,

and spread your protection over them,
that those who love your name may exult in you.
For you bless the righteous, O LORD;
you cover him with favor as with a shield.
(Ps. 5:11–12)

"Because the poor are plundered, because the needy
     groan,
I will now arise," says the LORD;
"I will place him in the safety for which he longs."
(Ps. 12:5)

Cast your burden on the LORD,
and he will sustain you;
he will never permit
the righteous to be moved. (Ps. 55:22)

O you who love the LORD, hate evil!
He preserves the lives of his saints;
he delivers them from the hand of the wicked.
Light is sown for the righteous,
and joy for the upright in heart.
Rejoice in the LORD, O you righteous,
and give thanks to his holy name! (Ps. 97:10–12)

The LORD protects the simple-hearted; when I was in
great need, he saved me. (Ps. 116:6 NIV)

The LORD watches over all who love him, but all the
wicked he will destroy. (Ps. 145:20 NIV)

The name of the LORD is a strong tower;
the righteous man runs into it and is safe.
(Prov. 18:10)

But the Lord is faithful. He will establish you and
guard you against the evil one. (2 Thess. 3:3)

The Blessing of Marriage, Sex, and Children

Therefore a man shall leave his father and his mother
and hold fast to his wife, and they shall become one
flesh. And the man and his wife were both naked and
were not ashamed. (Gen. 2:24–25)

You fill their womb with treasure;
they are satisfied with children,
and they leave their abundance to their infants.
(Ps. 17:14)

Behold, children are a heritage from the LORD,
the fruit of the womb a reward.
Like arrows in the hand of a warrior
are the children of one's youth.
Blessed is the man
who fills his quiver with them! (Ps. 127:3–5)

Let your fountain be blessed,
and rejoice in the wife of your youth,
a lovely deer, a graceful doe.
Let her breasts fill you at all times with delight;
be intoxicated always in her love. (Prov. 5:18–19)

Grandchildren are the crown of the aged,
and the glory of children is their fathers. (Prov. 17:6)

He who finds a wife finds a good thing
and obtains favor from the Lord. (Prov. 18:22)

Many waters cannot quench love,
neither can floods drown it.
If a man offered for love
all the wealth of his house,
he would be utterly despised. (Song of Sol. 8:7)

The husband should give to his wife her conjugal
rights, and likewise the wife to her husband. For the
wife does not have authority over her own body, but
the husband does. Likewise the husband does not
have authority over his own body, but the wife does.
(1 Cor. 7:3–4)

God's Promise of Provisions

You shall remember the LORD your God, for it is
he who gives you power to get wealth, that he may
confirm his covenant that he swore to your fathers, as
it is this day. (Deut. 8:18)

Therefore keep the words of this covenant and do
them, that you may prosper in all that you do.
(Deut. 29:9)

Jabez called upon the God of Israel, saying, "Oh that
you would bless me and enlarge my border, and that

your hand might be with me, and that you would keep
me from harm so that it might not bring me pain!"
And God granted what he asked. (1 Chron. 4:10)

Then you will prosper if you are careful to observe
the statutes and the rules that the LORD commanded
Moses for Israel. Be strong and courageous. Fear not;
do not be dismayed. (1 Chron. 22:13)

His delight is in the law of the LORD,
and on his law he meditates day and night.

He is like a tree
planted by streams of water
that yields its fruit in its season,
and its leaf does not wither.
In all that he does, he prospers. (Ps. 1:2–3)

The righteous shall inherit the land
and dwell upon it forever. (Ps. 37:29)

The righteous flourish like the palm tree
and grow like a cedar in Lebanon.
They are planted in the house of the LORD;
they flourish in the courts of our God. (Ps. 92:12–13)

Honor the LORD with your wealth
and with the first fruits of all your produce;
then your barns will be filled with plenty,
and your vats will be bursting with wine.
(Prov. 3:9–10)

Commit your work to the LORD,
and your plans will be established. (Prov. 16:3)

Bring the full tithe into the storehouse, that there may be food in my house. And thereby put me to the test, says the LORD of hosts, if I will not open the windows of heaven for you and pour down for you a blessing until there is no more need. (Mal. 3:10)

Look at the birds of the air: they neither sow nor reap nor gather into barns, and yet your heavenly Father feeds them. Are you not of more value than they? And which of you by being anxious can add a single hour to his span of life? And why are you anxious about clothing? Consider the lilies of the field, how they grow: they neither toil nor spin, yet I tell you, even Solomon in all his glory was not arrayed like one of these. But if God so clothes the grass of the field, which today is alive and tomorrow is thrown into the oven, will he not much more clothe you, O you of little faith? Therefore do not be anxious, saying, "What shall we eat?" or "What shall we drink?" or "What shall we wear?" For the Gentiles seek after all these things, and your heavenly Father knows that you need them all. But seek first the kingdom of God and his righteousness, and all these things will be added to you. (Matt. 6:26–33)

Give, and it will be given to you. Good measure, pressed down, shaken together, running over, will be

put into your lap. For with the measure you use it will
be measured back to you. (Luke 6:38)

Endnotes

1. Sowing Circle, Inc., *Blue Letter Bible*, "Greek Lexicon::G4053 (KJV)," accessed February 9, 2013, http://www.blueletterbible.org/lang/lexicon/lexicon.cfm?Strongs=G4053&t=KJV.

2. John Piper, *Fifty Reason Why Jesus Came to Die* (Wheaton, IL: Crossway Books, 2006), 43.

3. "Randy Alcorn: 'The Treasure Principle,'" Christian Broadcasting Network, accessed February 2, 2013, http://www.cbn.com/700club/Guests/Bios/Randy_Alcorn072205.aspx.

Chapter

9

Earn This

Another one of my favorite actors is the illustrious Tom Hanks. He has played several iconic roles during his successful Hollywood career; but his most epic performance was in the 1998 blockbuster, *Saving Private Ryan*, an impressive war film set during the Invasion of Normandy by the Allied Forces in World War II.

In this movie, General George Marshall discovers that three of the four young men from the Ryan family have all died in the war, and their mother has been informed of all three deaths on the same day. He also learns that the fourth son, Private First Class James Francis Ryan, is still serving but is currently missing in action. Private Ryan is the last remaining living male from the Ryan family. General Marshall is determined to send at least one of the Ryan men back home alive. A team is dispatched to find and rescue Private Ryan.

Tom Hanks plays Captain John H. Miller, the commander for Charlie Company, Second Ranger Battalion. He is called upon to lead the small group of men being dispatched to rescue Private Ryan with no information about Ryan's whereabouts. However, against the most incredible odds and after much toil and sacrifice, they do indeed eventually find Private Ryan. Captain Miller's crew joins Ryan and two other soldiers for one final epic battle to protect a bridge from German capture. Miller's team knows that holding the bridge could greatly help the Allied Forces.

Miller's team accomplish a mission that appeared to be impossible, successfully holding off the Germans and preserving the bridge for the allies! But the military win does not come without great costs. Several of the men in Miller's crew die in the battle, including Captain Miller himself. But Private Ryan survives. Miller's sacrifice, as well as the sacrifice of his team, allows Private Ryan to eventually make it back home safely.

Just a few moments away from breathing his last breath, Captain Miller has a brief dialogue with Private Ryan. Miller grabs Ryan's shirt to pull him close and then he makes this dying declaration: "Earn this!"

The movie ends with a flash forward to an elderly James Ryan kneeling and crying at the grave of Captain John Miller at Normandy American Cemetery and Memorial. And with him are his wife, his children, and his grandchildren. He pleads with his wife to confirm that he has been a good man. It appears that

Ryan has been consumed with living a life worthy of the sacrifice that Captain Miller and the other men made for him. By the loyalty his family is demonstrating, it appears the James Ryan has indeed been a decent husband and father. He has made the most of the gift that he had been given. The Ryan family legacy has continued, thanks to the sacrifice of the great men who laid down their lives for Private First Class James Francis Ryan.

When Captain Miller said those words, "Earn this!" he was calling Private Ryan to go do something with this. The men of Miller's crew had already died; they had already sacrificed to save Ryan's life. Now Miller was challenging Ryan to go live a life worthy of this sacrifice. To live his life in honor of what these men had chosen to do on his behalf. In essence, Captain John Miller was saying, "Ryan, don't waste this!"

The same is true with Christ. He is calling us to "Earn this!" Now, we know that we cannot ever earn salvation. We cannot do enough good works in our lives to earn the love of God demonstrated through the cross. But, why not try? Jesus has done so much for us; why not seek to live for him? Why not live life on mission?

Jesus has paid the penalty for our sin, but he isn't demanding we pay it back; he knows we couldn't ever pay it back. But why not live a life seeking to honor him? We seek to live righteously, not because we feel obligated to, but because we are so grateful for God's grace in our lives. Jesus Christ has already died and risen again. He already redeemed us. He already made the sacrifices. Now let's go live a life worthy of the

> Jesus has paid the penalty for our sin, but he isn't demanding we pay it back.

sacrifice! Let's not waste what we have been given. The Apostle Paul encourages us in this regard:

> I press on toward the goal for the prize of the upward call of God in Christ Jesus. Let those of us who are mature think this way, and if in anything you think otherwise, God will reveal that also to you. Only let us hold true to what we have attained. (Phil. 3:14–16)

> I therefore, a prisoner for the Lord, urge you to walk in a manner worthy of the calling to which you have been called, with all humility and gentleness, with patience, bearing with one another in love, eager to maintain the unity of the Spirit in the bond of peace. (Eph. 4:1–3)

We've already obtained this salvation. We have already been rescued. Let us then "press on toward the goal." Let's live up to the calling that he has placed on our lives. Let's maximize the liberty we have been given. We are already righteous, so let's go live righteously!

Making the Most of the Moment

In the spring of 2002, I was a student at a ministry training program at a large church in Northern Illinois. One of the requirements of graduating from the program was going on a mission trip. In order to be a part of the trip, I had to fundraise seventeen hundred dollars. Due to my financial situation, this was a very difficult task, particularly considering I was barely able to pay my tuition to remain in the program.

As the financial deadline approached, I had only raised a few hundred dollars toward my trip. But the day before we had to have all our money in, the director of the missions department, Sean Kelly, approached me. He told me that someone had approached him with a donation of twelve hundred dollars. The person instructed Sean to give it to whatever student had worked hard to fundraise but was still struggling financially. Sean selected me and credited my account with the full donation.

I remember the moment Sean told me; I fell to my knees crying, filled with joy and gratitude, toward both the anonymous benefactor and toward Sean. Two people had made it possible for me to take part in a trip that I both needed and desperately wanted. I also vividly remember thinking to myself, "I'm going to live up to this!"

Someone had made a large donation on my behalf, and Sean had believed in me enough to allow me to go on that trip. I didn't want their sacrifice and confidence in me to go to waste. The only appropriate response was to make it a great trip. I didn't have the ability to earn what they had done for me, but I could make sure I got the most of the trip. Every day of that mission trip, I woke up saying to myself, "I'm going to make Sean proud." I maximized that trip. I talked to every person I could, I served with all my heart, I gave it 100 percent of my effort, all day every day! I sought to live up to that which I had already received. I sought to make the most of the moment.

And this is what we ought to do in our lives, with God. We have already been granted these amazing gifts and provisions by God. Why not seek to make the most of them? Why not live a life worthy of the calling we have received?

I don't want the sacrifice of Christ to be a waste in my life. If he died to make me righteous, then I want to wholeheartedly embrace being righteous. If he suffered so that I could enjoy being Abba's child, then I want to enjoy being Abba's child every minute of every day. If Jesus was brutally beaten and horrifically murdered for my freedom and my redemption, I want to maximize the life and liberty I have been given. Why not make the most of the things that he purchased for us? Why not?!

How Do We Earn This?

Let me make it clear, when I say "earn this," I am speaking metaphorically. We cannot ever earn grace. Nothing we can do could ever merit God's favor.

When I say "earn this," I mean living a life to honor the sacrifice Christ made; and living a life that allows other people to see Christ in me. Jesus has wonderfully written my story of rescue and redefinition. He has now invited me to be a part of the story of coming to know Jesus, being rescued and redefined. If I choose to answer his call, I can be a part of the story he is writing in the lives of other people.

> Before your transformation, you had no choice but to continually sin. But now, you can have victory over sin!

How do we do this? How do we honor Christ? How do we live our lives in such a way that others will see Jesus shining in us? Simple. Holiness! Seek to be holy. Get rid of anything that does not glorify God! God calls us to be holy:

> Do not be conformed to the passions of your former
> ignorance, but as he who called you is holy, you also
> be holy in all your conduct, since it is written, "You
> shall be holy, for I am holy." (1 Pet. 1:14–16)

Before your transformation, you had no choice but to continually sin. But now, you can have victory over sin! You have been set free from its power. You no longer have to go on living your old life. You can break free:

> For sin will have no dominion over you, since you are
> not under law but under grace.
>   What then? Are we to sin because we are not
> under law but under grace? By no means! Do you
> not know that if you present yourselves to anyone
> as obedient slaves, you are slaves of the one whom
> you obey, either of sin, which leads to death, or of
> obedience, which leads to righteousness? But thanks
> be to God, that you who were once slaves of sin have
> become obedient from the heart to the standard
> of teaching to which you were committed, and,
> having been set free from sin, have become slaves of
> righteousness. (Rom. 6:14–18)

We are no longer slaves to sin. God has set us free from the power of sin. He empowers us and expects us to allow sanctification to be at work in our lives.

God hates sin! Sin separated God from his beloved creation (see Isa. 59:2). It brought death into the world (see Rom. 5:12). It devastates our lives. It continually destroys churches, families, and destinies. I heard a preacher once say, "Sin will take you further than you want to go; cost you more than you want to pay; and keep you longer than you want to stay."

God is inviting us to be holy! Calling us to be different. Through Christ we can righteously stand out from the crowd. We are called to do whatever it takes to live righteous lives and to be different from those around us:

> For God has not called us for impurity, but in holiness. Therefore whoever disregards this, disregards not man but God, who gives his Holy Spirit to you. (1 Thess. 4:7–8)

If you ignore holiness, you are blatantly ignoring God. We are called to rid ourselves of impurity, to be holy. We are called to conduct ourselves in the right manner. Sin runs rampant in the culture around us. We are called to be different than the sinners of the world.

As you seek to be holy every day, you may not be perfect in your battle against sin, but certainly you ought to win more battles than you lose. And most certainly you ought to become more like Jesus Christ each day. You ought to sin less today than you did yesterday. And you ought to sin less tomorrow than you did today. Some people say that's an unrealistic goal. But I'd ask why?! If the Holy Spirit is in us at all times, that means we are always equipped to overcome sin.

One of the main goals of our lives ought to be to defeat sin, each and every time it rears its ugly head. Of course, this can only be accomplished through the grace of God. Grace means that you are getting something you did not earn. When God declares you righteous, that is grace manifested in your life. You have a status pronounced upon you that you did not earn. However, the grace to defeat sin is the intrinsic form of grace. You are given an empowerment that you did not earn. God freely bestows his grace to you, allowing you to accomplish things that you otherwise would have been incapable of doing. This is what allows us to see victory over sin. The Apostle Paul wrote these words to Titus:

> For the grace of God has appeared, bringing salvation for all people, training us to renounce ungodliness and worldly passions, and to live self-controlled, upright, and godly lives in the present age, waiting for our blessed hope, the appearing of the glory of our great God and Savior Jesus Christ, who gave himself for us to redeem us from all lawlessness and to purify for himself a people for his own possession who are zealous for good works.
>
> Declare these things; exhort and rebuke with all authority. Let no one disregard you. (2:11–15)

God is preparing us to do mighty things, giving us the grace to be effective in service to his kingdom. As God sanctifies us, we become more righteous in our actions and more zealous in our desires to good things for God. Before you were saved, you weren't passionate about evangelism or missions or serving the needy or helping the poor; but now that you have a new heart, now that you've had the grace of God bestowed to you, you love to see others hear about Jesus and you love to serve people in their need. This is made possible by grace.

The Apostle Paul understood that he could not be effective in life or in ministry unless the grace of God was granted to him:

> But by the grace of God I am what I am, and his grace toward me was not in vain. On the contrary, I worked harder than any of them, though it was not I, but the grace of God that is with me. Whether then it was I or they, so we preach and so you believed. (1 Cor. 15:10–11)

God grants us the grace to defeat sin, to live holy lives, and to be effective in ministry. God goes even further, always giving us a way out when we are tempted. Some people say, "I can't stop sinning." That is nonsense! Every time you are tempted to sin, there is a way out:

> No temptation has overtaken you that is not common to man. God is faithful, and he will not let you be tempted beyond your ability, but with the temptation he will also provide the way of escape, that you may be able to endure it. (1 Cor. 10:13)

God only allows temptations to come your way to which you have it in you to say "No!" Again, it's not your power but the power of God living in you.

God makes a way out of every temptation. If God is making a way out of each and *every* opportunity to sin, then it's obvious to me that he is looking for us to actually take that way out, every time.

Now, of course, this is why grace is so great. If we don't take the way out, he still loves us! Our status as his child is not affected or negated. Our report cards remain unblemished, no matter what choice we make.

But why wouldn't we want to defeat sin? I love God and I know he hates sin. And because I love God, I want to uphold the things he loves and I want to destroy the things he hates. The Holy Spirit is at work in our lives. We have everything we need to live righteously and experience the abundant life God desires for us:

> As we engage in this war against sin, God will empower us.

> His divine power has granted to us all things that pertain to life and godliness, through the knowledge of him who called us to his own glory and excellence, by which he has granted to us his precious and very great promises, so that through them you may become partakers of the divine nature, having escaped from the corruption that is in the world because of sinful desire. (2 Pet. 1:3–4)

We have everything we need to be godly people. We have the power of God. Let's overcome sin. Let's destroy it. Let's live righteously!

It's Time to Make War

Now, it won't always be easy to fight sin. Sometimes overcoming sin can be difficult if you've developed bad habits and addictions. This is literally a war! But the good news is that the outcome of this war has already been determined. *We win!*

As we engage in this war against sin, God will empower us.

So many Christians allow sin and strongholds to remain in their lives—they do not get serious enough. God desires we wage war against the sin that harms us. Pastor and author John Piper made this bold statement:

> The only possible attitude towards out-of-control desire is a declaration of all-out war. I hear so many Christians murmuring about their imperfections and their failures and their addictions and their shortcomings, and I see so little war! "Murmur, murmur, murmur, why am I this way?" MAKE WAR! If you wonder how to make war, go to the manual. Don't just bellyache about your failures. MAKE WAR! There is something about war that sharpens the senses . . . there is a mean violent streak to the true Christian life, violence against whom or what? Not other people, but a violence, a mean streak, against our own selves and all in us that would make peace with sin. It's a violence against all lusts in ourselves, all enslaving desires . . . this is our enemy. This is where we MAKE WAR![1]

God wants us to get serious about getting rid of sin. He is serious about us being holy. We have undergone a radical transformation and we are now called to live a life above the norm. It's time to put some things into place in your life so that you can be disciplined in your quest for holiness. It's time to make war! Think about Olympic athletes or professional sports players. They have a goal in mind and they go into strict training to put themselves into position to reach their goal. Many of them train their whole lives. They change their diets, they take special vitamins and supplements, they deny themselves certain foods they may want, and they spend countless hours in the gym training and getting strong. Many athletes spend hours in film sessions studying their opponents, seeking how to exploit their opponents' weaknesses, and many more spend hours with their coaches learning how to be better in their quest for the prize.

The Apostle Paul equates what athletes do with what we ought to do:

> Every athlete exercises self-control in all things.
> They do it to receive a perishable wreath, but we an
> imperishable. So I do not run aimlessly; I do not box
> as one beating the air. But I discipline my body and
> keep it under control, lest after preaching to others I
> myself should be disqualified. (1 Cor. 9:25–27)

Think about all the work athletes invest. All of that to receive a prize that will only last a short time. But we are seeking to win a prize that will last for all of eternity! How much more should we go into strict training? How much harder should we work?

We ought to be running hard in our pursuit for holiness our entire lives. We ought to go on a "spiritual diet," being cautious of what we allow our minds and hearts to consume. We ought to work hard to get strong in our faith. We ought to know how to exploit our opponent's weakness (our opponent, of course, is the devil). And we ought to spend countless hours with our coach, as he will teach us and empower us in our quest for holiness.

Jesus was very serious about us going into strict training so that we can live holy lives and get rid of sin. He gave his disciples this firm advice:

> You have heard that it was said, "You shall not commit adultery." But I say to you that everyone who looks at a woman with lustful intent has already committed adultery with her in his heart. If your right eye causes you to sin, tear it out and throw it away. For it is better that you lose one of your members than that your whole body be thrown into hell. And if your right hand causes you to sin, cut it off and throw it away. For it is better that you lose one of your members than that your whole body go into hell. (Matt. 5:27–30)

Tough words from our Lord! This demonstrates the seriousness with which we ought to approach sin. Whatever is going to cause you to sin must be "cut off." That means relationships, media, hobbies, or whatever—anything that causes you to sin, get rid of it!

Let us go into strict training so that we can run the race well—the race that God has marked out for us:

> Therefore, since we are surrounded by such a great cloud of witnesses, let us throw off everything that hinders and the sin that so easily entangles, and let us run with perseverance the race marked out for us. Let us fix our eyes on Jesus, the author and perfecter of our faith, who for the joy set before him

endured the cross, scorning its shame, and sat down at the right hand of the throne of God. Consider him who endured such opposition from sinful men, so that you will not grow weary and lose heart. (Heb. 12:1–3 NIV)

> Run hard after God. Run hard after holiness! Seek to get rid of *all* sin.

Run hard after God. Run hard after holiness! Seek to get rid of *all* sin. Initially, you may not be perfect in your battle against sin, but you certainly will win more battles than you lose. As you go into strict training, you get stronger. As you mature in your faith, your ability to be holy will grow stronger. You will win more battles today than you did yesterday . . . and certainly you will win more battles tomorrow than you did today.

Even when we fail in our quest for holiness, even when we blow it big, we can still be confident in his love and approval for us. When we fail, we know that we still have the imputed righteousness on our record, and that even our own failures do not impede our status as righteous in his sight. So when we fail, we just get back up and keep going. No need to feel guilty. Just like a horse rider ought to do when he gets thrown off, we simply brush the dust off and we get back on:

> For the righteous falls seven times and rises again,
> but the wicked stumble in times of calamity.
> (Prov. 24:16)

No matter how many times you fall, you can get back up. That's what righteous people do. They get back up and keep fighting.

As you war against sin—and toward a greater love for God—it is imperative to always remember that you are fighting to defeat sin from a position of supernatural victory that has already been obtained for you. You are not fighting to gain the ability to overcome sin. Before salvation, you were enslaved to sin and had no chance to overcome it. Today, you have a new nature and you will be successful as you fight against sin.

Let us make war against our sin. Let's chase holiness! Let's make war against anything that does not honor Christ. Let us go into strict training so that we might defeat sin. Let us be ferocious in our fight against sin and let us be relentless in our pursuit of holiness. Let us seek to run the race that the Lord has marked out for us. This quest will be hard, but it will be worth it.

With confidence in our transformation and in the exchange orchestrated by God, we can run hard after holiness and we can be intimate with the Almighty. We can be fully satisfied in him because we have been redefined.

Jesus has already done the work for us, already done the heavy lifting. He did all the work at the cross. Let us live righteously, not because we have to but because we get to. God has imputed us with his own righteousness! God has given us his grace! Let's run after Jesus with everything we've got inside of us. Let's live this life on mission, so that the glory of God will shine in us and through us.

We are righteous. We are justified. We have been adopted into his royal family. We are citizens of heaven and guaranteed many blessings. We have been rescued. We have been redefined! We are loved! *LET'S GO SHOW THE WORLD WHO OUR GOD IS!*

Endnote

1. "Make War!!! (John Piper)," 1031 Sermon Jams, uploaded September 1, 2008, accessed September 23, 2012, http://www.youtube.com/watch?v=GhAeIjFngyE.

About the Author

Kenneth Ortiz is passionately committed to articulating the depths of God's fierce love. He is a dynamic communicator with a bold but conversational style of speaking and writing. Kenneth is a gifted Bible teacher and expositor, often using relevant illustrations that deeply resonate with audiences and readers. His words are always laced with incredible humor and friendly intimacy.

Born and raised in Philadelphia, Pennsylvania, Kenneth was raised in a home where neither one of his parents followed Jesus, so he had little knowledge of God. Not too long after his parents' bitter divorce, Kenneth met a friend who invited him to church. He attended church regularly for a few months and eventually, at the age of fourteen, he made a commitment to follow Jesus. He quickly became a young, radical preaching machine, and as a teenager, he developed an incredible knack for using great illustrations to articulate the profound truths he was learning.

After graduating from Central High School, Kenneth received two years of ministry training at the Rockford Master's Commission (now known as FocusOne) in Rockford, Illinios. After his time in Rockford, he entered full-time vocational pastoral ministry.

Over the past ten years, Kenneth has been a youth pastor, evangelist, freelance writer, and successful entrepreneur. Through these life experiences, he discovered a tragic trend: many Christians live far beneath God's greatest potential. This discovery inspired Kenneth to begin speaking boldly to audiences about the benefits of thoroughly understanding the depths of God's immutable love.

As an itinerant evangelist, Kenneth has traveled extensively, speaking and preaching to audiences of all ages. He has preached to more than eighty-five thousand people over the past several years. He currently lives in Winter Garden, Florida, where he serves as a member of the ministry staff team of Mosaic Church. Kenneth has earned a bachelor's degree in Psychology and is currently pursuing a graduate degree in Theological Studies. He has been an ordained minister since 2006.

Contact the Author:

Web: www.kennethortiz.com

Twitter: @kennethortiz